MY LIFE IN THE SOUTH

THIRD EDITION.

MY LIFE IN THE SOUTH.

By

JACOB STROYER.

NEW AND ENGLARGED EDITION

SALEM.

SALEM OBSERVER BOOK AND JOB PRINT,

1885.

MY LIFE IN THE SOUTH

By Jacob Stroyer

As Published in 1885

Trade Paperback ISBN: 1-58218-718-5
Hardcover ISBN: 1-58218-719-3
eBook ISBN: 1-58218-717-7

Digital Scanning and Publishing is a leader in the electronic republication of historical books and documents. We publish many of our titles as eBooks, as well as traditional hardcover and trade paper editions. DSI is committed to bringing many traditional and little known books back to life, retaining the look and feel of the original work.

Cover artwork from *The Life and Times of Frederick Douglas* by Frederick Douglas as published in 1882.

First DSI Printing: June 2001

Published by DIGITAL SCANNING, INC.
Scituate, MA 02066
Toll Free: 888-349-4443
Outside U.S.: 781-545-2100

www.digitalscanning.com

INTRODUCTION.

SALEM, AUGUST 4, 1879.

I have read the manuscript from which this little work by Rev. Mr. Stroyer is printed and found it both interesting and instructive. It is in simple style and words, the autobiography of an emancipated slave, born and raised on an extensive plantation in central South Carolina, the owner of which had on his own several plantations, nearly 500 negroes of varying shades of complexion, all becoming free men by the Proclamation in 1864. The writer, now (1879), minister of the African Methodist Episcopal Church in this city, tells of his own severe training and experience, of some of the customary ways of owners and of slaves – of the severity of plantation discipline, and of the burdens of a life of involuntary servitude. Hints are not wanting that the importation of slaves was not, in the time of the author, wholly discontinued.

The hope of Mr. Stroyer is that he may be able, by the sale of his work, to raise means to enable him to add to an education already attained with very great difficulty and long and patient toil and waiting, his whole object being to devote his services and attainments to the good of his race.

HENRY K. OLIVER.

AUGUST 13, 1879.

In this book Mr. Stroyer has given us, with a most simple and effective realism, the inside view of the institution of slavery. It is worth reading, to know how men, intelligent enough to report their experience, felt under the yoke. The time has come when American slavery can be studied historically, without passion, save such as mixes itself with the wonder that so great an evil could exist so long as a social form or a political idol. The time has not come when such study is unnecessary; for to deal justly by white or black in the United States, their previous relations must be understood, and nothing which casts light on the most universal and practical of those relations is without value to-day. I take pleasure therefore in saying that I consider Mr. Stroyer a competent and trustworthy witness to these details of plantation life.

E. C. BOLLES.

CITY OF SALEM, MAYOR'S OFFICE,
Nov. 5, 1884.

This is to certify that since the year 1876 I have known Rev. Jacob Stroyer, as a preacher and minister to the colored people of this city. He is earnest, devoted and faithful.

He is endeavoring by the sale of this book to realize the means to enable him by a course of study, to better fit himself as a minister to preach in the South.

I most cheerfully commend him in his praiseworthy efforts.

WM. M. HILL, *Mayor.*

City of Salem, Mass.,
Mayor's Office, Jan. 20, 1885.

Such tales as Mr. Stroyer's are now no longer required to enlighten the community and show the few lights and many shadows of American slavery. We may be thankful that the subject has now simply an historical interest.

Although it does not possess the dramatic incidents of Mrs. Stowe's famous story, it has the advantage of being a true sketch of Southern life. It is a simple, readable production, and shows what education will do for the race.

Mr. Stroyer will do good work among his people, and deserves encouragement and support.

Arthur L. Huntington, *Mayor.*

Mr. Stroyer's book is a setting forth in a fresh and unique manner of the old and bitter wrongs of American Slavery. It is an inside view of a phase of our national life which has happily passed away forever. Although it concerns itself largely with incidents and details, it is not without the historical value which attaches to reliable personal reminiscences. The author has made commendable progress in intellectual culture, and is worthy of generous assistance in his effort to fit himself still more perfectly for labor among his needy brethren in the South.

E. S. ATWOOD.

PREFACE.

THIRD EDITION.

The author, in presenting the third edition of his book to the public, would take occasion to thank his patrons for the very liberal manner in which they have appreciated his efforts. When the work was first projected, the necessity for another edition was not thought of; but the unexpected favor which the work has met at the hands of those interested in the author and his object, has constrained him to offer a second and now a third edition of this little story of the trials and sufferings of himself and his once oppressed brethren, to their kind consideration.

J. S.

CHAPTER I

CHAPTER I.

My father was born in Sierra Leone, Africa. Of his parents and his brothers and sisters I know nothing. I only remember that it was said that his father's name was Moncoso, and his mother's Mongomo, which names are known only among the native Africans. He was brought from Africa when but a boy, and sold to old Colonel Dick Singleton, who owned a great many plantations in South Carolina, and when the old colonel divided his property among his children, father fell to the second son, Col. M.R. Singleton.

Mother never was sold, but her parents were; they were owned by one Mr. Crough, who sold them and the rest of the slaves, with the plantation, to Col. Dick Singleton, upon whose place mother was born. I was born on this extensive plantation, twenty-eight miles southeast of Columbia, South Carolina, in the year 1849. I belonged to Col. M.R. Singleton, and was held in slavery up to the time of the emancipation proclamation issued by President Lincoln.

THE CHILDREN.

My father had fifteen children: four boys and three girls by his first wife and eight by his second. Their names were as follows: of the boys--Toney, Aszerine, Duke and Dezine; of the girls--Violet, Priscilla, and Lydia. Those of his second wife were as follows: Footy, Embrus, Caleb, Mitchell, Cuffey and Jacob, and of the girls, Catherine and Retta.

SAND HILL DAYS.

Col. M.R. Singleton was like many other rich slave owners in the South, who had summer seats four, six or eight miles from the plantation, where they carried the little negro boys and girls too small to work.

Our summer seat, or the sand hill, as the slaves used to call it, was four miles from the plantation. Among the four hundred and sixty-five slaves owned by the colonel there were a great many children. If my readers had visited Col. Singleton's plantation the last of May or the first of June in the days of slavery, they would have seen three or four large plantation wagons loaded with little negroes of both sexes, of various complexions and conditions, who were being carried to this summer residence, and among them they would have found the author of this little work in his sand-hill days.

My readers would naturally ask how many seasons these children were taken to the summer seats? I answer, until, in the judgment of the overseer, they were large enough to work; then they were kept at the plantation. How were they fed? There were three or four women who were too old to work on the plantation who were sent as nurses to the summer seats with the children; they did the cooking. The way in which these old women cooked for 80, and sometimes 150 children, in my sand-hill days, was this:--they had two or three large pots, which held about a bushel each, in which they used to cook corn flour, stirred with large wooden paddles. The food was dealt out with the paddles into each child's little wooden tray or tin pail, which was furnished by the parents according to their ability.

With this corn flour, which the slaves called mush, each child used to get a gill of sour milk brought daily from the plantation in a large wooden pail on the head of a boy or man. We children used to like the sour milk, or hard clabber as it was called by the slaves; but that seldom changed diet, namely the mush, was hated worse than medicine. Our hatred was increased against the mush from the fact that they used to give us molasses to eat with it, instead of clabber. The hateful mixture made us anxious for Sundays to come, when our mothers, fathers, sisters and brothers would bring something from the plantation, which, however poor, we considered very nice, compared with what we had during the week days. Among the many desirable things our parents brought us the most delightful was cow pease, rice, and a piece of bacon, cooked together; the mixture was called by the slaves "hopping John."

THE STORY OF GILBERT.

A few large boys were sent yearly to the sand-hill among the smaller ones, as guides. At the time to which I am referring there was one by the name of Gilbert, who used to go around with the smaller boys in the woods to gather bushes and sticks for the old women to cook our food with.

Gilbert was a cruel boy. He used to strip his little fellow negroes while in the woods, and whip them two or three times a week, so that their backs were all scarred, and threatened them with severer punishment if they told; this state of things had been going on for quite a while. As I was a favorite with Gilbert, I always had managed to escape a whipping, with the promise of keeping the secret of the punishment of the rest, which I did, not so much that I was afraid of Gilbert, as because I always was inclined to mind my own business. But finally, one day, Gilbert said to me, "Jake," as he used to call me, "you am a good boy, but I'm gwine to wip you some to-day, as I wip dem toder boys." Of course I was required to strip off my only garment, which was an Osnaburg linen shirt, worn by both sexes of the negro children in the summer. As I stood trembling before my merciless superior, who had a switch in his hand, thousands of thoughts went through my little mind as to how to get rid of the whipping. I finally fell upon a plan which I hoped would save me from a punishment that was near at hand. There were some carpenters in the woods, some distance from us, hewing timber; they were far away, but it was a clear morning, so we could hear their voices and the sound of the axes. Having resolved in my mind what I would do. I commenced reluctantly to take off my shirt, at the same time pleading with Gilbert, who paid no attention to my prayer, but said, "Jake, I is gwine to wip you to-day as I did dem toder boys." Having satisfied myself that no mercy was to be found with Gilbert, I drew my shirt off and threw it over his head, and bounded forward on a run in the direction of the sound of the carpenters. By the time he got from the entanglement of my garment, I had quite a little start of him. Between my starting point and the place where the carpenters were at work I jumped over some bushes five or six feet high. Gilbert soon gained upon me, and sometimes touched me with his hands, but as I had on nothing for him to hold to, he could not take hold of me. As I began to come in sight of the carpenters, Gilbert begged me not to go to them, for he knew that it would be bad for him, but as that was not a time for me to listen to his entreaties, I moved on faster. As I got near to the carpenters, one of them ran and met me, into whose arms I jumped. The man into whose arms I ran was Uncle Benjamin, my mother's uncle. As he clasped me in his arms, he said, "Bres de Lo, my son, wat is de matter?" But I was so exhausted that it was quite a while before I could tell him my trouble; when recovered from my breathless condition, I told him that Gilbert had been in the habit of stripping the boys and whipping them two or three times a week, when we went into the woods, and threatened them with greater punishment if they told. I said he had never whipped me before, but I was cautioned to keep the secret, which I had done up to this time; but he said he was going to whip me this morning, so I threw my shirt over his head and ran here for protection. Gilbert did not follow me after I got in sight of the carpenters, but sneaked away. Of course my body was all bruised and scratched by the bushes. Acting as a guide for Uncle Benjamin, I took him to where I had left my garment.

At this time the children were scattered around in the woods, waiting for what the trouble would bring; They all were gathered up and taken to the sand-hill house, examined, and it was found, as I have stated, that their backs were all scarred. Gilbert was brought to trial, severely whipped, and they made him beg all the children to pardon him for his treatment to them. But he never was allowed to go into the woods with the rest of the children during that season. My sand-hill associates always thanked me for the course I took, which saved them and myself from further punishment by him.

MASTER AND MISTRESS VISITING.

When master and mistress were to visit their little negroes at the sand-hill, the news was either brought by the overseer who resided at the above named place, and went back and forth to the plantation, or by one of master's house servants, a day ahead. The preparation required to receive our white guests was that each little negro was to be washed, and clad in the best dress he or she had. But before this was done, the unsuccessful attempt was made to straighten out our unruly wools with some small cards, or Jim-Crows as we called them.

On one occasion an old lady, by the name of Janney Cuteron, attempted to straighten out my wool with one of those Jim-crows; as she hitched the teeth of the instrument in my unyielding wool with her great masculine hand, of course I was jerked flat on my back. This was the common fate of most of my associates, whose wools were of the same nature, but with a little water and the strong application of the Jim-crow, the old lady soon combed out my wool into some sort of shape.

As our preparations were generally completed three-quarters of an hour before our guests came, we were placed in line, the boys together and the girls by themselves. We were then drilled in the art of addressing our expected visitors. The boys were required to bend the body forward with head down, and rest the body on the left foot, and scrape the right foot backward on the ground, while uttering the words, "how dy Massie and Missie." The girls were required to use the same words, accompanied with a courtesy. But when Master and Mistress had left, the little African wools were neglected until the news of their next visit.

Our sand-hill days were very pleasant, outside of the seldom changed diet, namely the mush, which we had sometimes to eat with molasses, the treatment of Gilbert, and the attempt to straighten out our unruly wools.

I said that my father was brought from Africa when but a boy, and was sold to old Col. Dick Singleton; and when the children were of age, the Colonel divided his plantations among them, and father fell to Col. M.K. Singleton, who was the second son.

On this large plantation there were 465 slaves; there were not so many when it was given to Col. M.R., but increased to the above stated number, up to the time of emancipation.

My father was not a field hand; my first recollection of him was that he used to take care of hogs and cows in the swamp, and when too old for that work he was sent to the plantation to take care of horses and mules, as master had a great many for the use of his farm.

I have stated that father said that his father's name in Africa was Moncoso, and his mother's Mongomo, but I never learned what name he went by before he was brought to this country. I only know that he stated that Col. Dick Singleton gave him the name of William, by which he was known up to the day of his death. Father had a surname, Stroyer, which he could not use in public, as the surname Stroyer would be against the law; he was known only by the name of William Singleton, because that was his master's name. So the title Stroyer was forbidden him, and could be used only by his children after the emancipation of the slaves.

There were two reasons given by the slave holders why they did not allow a slave to use his own name, but rather that of the master. The first was that, if he ran away, he would not be so easily detected by using his own name as by that of his master. The second was that to allow him to use his own name would be sharing an honor which was due only to his master, and that would be too much for a negro, said they, who was nothing more than a servant. So it was held as a crime for a slave to be caught using his own name, a crime which would expose him to severe punishment. But thanks be to God that those days have passed, and we now live under the sun of liberty.

MOTHER.

Mother's name was Chloe. She belonged to Col. M.R. Singleton too; she was a field hand, and never was sold, but her parents were once.

Mr. Crough who, as I have said had owned this plantation on which mother lived, had sold the plantation to Col. Dick Singleton, with mother's parents on it, before she was born.

Most of the family from which mother came, had trades of some kind; some were carpenters, some were blacksmiths, some house servants, and others were made drivers over the other negroes. Of course the negro drivers would be under a white man, who was called the overseer. Sometimes the negro drivers were a great deal worse to their fellow negroes than were the white men.

Mother had an uncle by the name of Esau, whom master thought more of than he did of the overseer. Uncle Esau was more cruel than was any white man master ever had on his plantation. Many of the slaves used to run away from him into the woods. I have known some of the negroes to run away from the cruel treatment of Uncle Esau, and to stay off eight or ten months. They were so afraid of him that they used to say that they would rather see the devil than to see him; they were glad when he died. But while so much was said of Uncle Esau, which was also true of many other negro drivers, the overseers themselves were not guiltless of cruelty to the defenceless slaves.

I have said that most of the family from which mother came had trades of some kind; but she had to take her chance in the field with those who had to weather the storm. But my readers are not to think that those whom I have spoken of as having trades were free from punishment, for they were not; some of them had more trouble than had the field hands. At times the overseer, who was a white man, would go to the shop of the blacksmith, or carpenter, and would pick a quarrel with him, so as to get an opportunity to punish him. He would say to the negro, "Oh, ye think yourself as good as ye master, ye--" Of course he knew what the overseer was after, so he was afraid to speak; the overseer, hearing no answer, would turn to him and cry out, "ye so big ye can't speak to me, ye--," and then the conflict would begin, and he would give that man such a punishment as would disable him for two or three months. The merciless overseer would say to him, "Ye think because ye have a trade ye are as good as ye master, ye--; but I will show ye that ye are nothing but a nigger."

I said that my father had two wives and fifteen children: four boys and three girls by the first, and six boys and two girls by the second wife. Of course he did not marry his wives as they do now, as it was not allowed among the slaves, but he took them as his wives by mutual agreement. He had my mother after the death of his first wife. I am the third son of his second wife.

My readers would very naturally like to know whether some of the slaves did not have more than one woman. I answer, they had; for as they had no law to bind them to one woman, they could have as many as they pleased by mutual agreement. But notwithstanding, they had a sense of the moral law, for many of them felt that it was right to have but one woman; they had different opinions about plurality of wives, as have the most educated and refined among the whites.

I met one of my fellow negroes one day, who lived next neighbor to us, and I said to him, "Well, Uncle William, how are you, to-day?" His answer was "Thank God, my son, I have two wives now, and must try and make out with them until I get some more." But while you will find many like him, others would rebuke the idea of having more than one wife. But, thanks be to God, the day has come when no one need to plead ignorance, for master and servant are both bound by the same law.

I did not go to the sand-hill, or summer seat, my alloted time, but stopped on the plantation with father, as I said that he used to take care of horses and mules. I was around with him in the barn yard when but a very small boy; of course that gave me an early relish for the occupation of hostler, and I soon made known my preference to Col. Singleton, who was a sportsman, and an owner of fine horses. And, although I was too small to work, the Colonel granted my request; hence I was allowed to be numbered among those who took care of the fine horses, and learned to ride. But I soon found that my new occupation demanded a little more than I cared for.

It was not long after I had entered my new work before they put me upon the back of a horse which threw me to the ground almost as soon as I had reached his back. It hurt me a little, but that was not the worst of it, for when I got up there was a man standing near with a switch, in hand, and he immediately began to beat me. Although I was a very bad boy, this was the first time I had been whipped by any one except father and mother, so I cried out in a tone of voice as if I would say, this is the first and last whipping you will give me when father gets hold of you.

When I had got away from him I ran to father with all my might, but soon found my expectation blasted, as father very coolly said to me, "Go back to your work and be a good boy, for I cannot do anything for you." But that did not satisfy me, so on I went to mother with my complaint and she came out to the man who had whipped me; he was a groom, a white man master had hired to train the horses. Mother and he began to talk, then he took a whip and started for her, and she ran from him, talking all the time. I ran back and forth between mother and him until he stopped beating her. After the fight between the groom and mother, he took me back to the stable yard and gave me a severe flogging. And, although mother failed to help me at first, still I had faith that when he had taken me back to the stable yard, and commenced whipping me, she would come and stop him, but I looked in vain, for she did not come.

Then the idea first came to me that I, with my dear father and mother and the rest of my fellow negroes, was doomed to cruel treatment through life, and was defenceless. But when I found that father and mother could not save me from punishment, as they themselves had to submit to the same treatment, I concluded to appeal to the sympathy of the groom, who seemed to have full control over me; but my pitiful cries never touched his sympathy, for things seemed to grow worse rather than better; so I made up my mind to stem the storm the best I could.

I have said that Col. Singleton had fine horses, which he kept for racing, and he owned two very noted ones, named Capt. Miner and Inspector. Perhaps some of my readers have already heard of Capt. Miner, for he was widely known, having won many races in Charlestown and Columbia, S.C., also in Augusta, Ga., and New York. He was a dark bay, with short tail. Inspector was a chestnut sorrel, and had the reputation of being a very great horse. These two horses have won many thousand dollars for the the colonel. I rode these two horses a great many times in their practice gallops, but never had the opportunity to ride them in a race before Col. Singleton died, for he did not live long after I had learned so that I could ride for money. The custom was, that when a boy had learned the trade of a rider, he would have to ride what was known as a trial, in the presence of a judge, who would approve or disapprove his qualifications to be admitted as a race rider, according to the jockey laws of South Carolina at that time.

I have said that I loved the business and acquired the skill very early, and this enabled me to pass my examination creditably, and to be accepted as a capable rider, but I passed through some very severe treatment before reaching that point.

This white man who trained horses for Col. Singleton was named Boney Young; he had a brother named Charles, who trained for the colonel's brother, John Singleton. Charles was a good man, but Boney our trainer, was as mean as Charles was good; he could smile in the face of one who was suffering the most painful death at his hands.

One day, about two weeks after Boney Young and mother had the conflict, he called me to him, as though he were in the pleasantest mood; he was singing. I ran to him as if to say by action, I will do anything you bid me, willingly. When I got to him he said, "Go and bring me a switch, sir." I answered, "yes, sir," and off I went and brought him one; then he said, "come in here, sir;" I answered, "yes, sir;" and I went into a horse's stall, but while I was going in a thousand thoughts passed through my mind as to what he wanted me to go into the stall for, but when I had got in I soon learned, for he gave me a first-class flogging.

A day or to after that he called me in the same way, and I went again, and he sent me for a switch. I brought him a short stubble that was worn out, which he took and beat me on the head with. Then he said to me, "Go and bring me a switch, sir;" I answered "Yes, sir;" and off I went the second time, and brought him one very little better than the first; he broke that over my head also, saying, "Go and bring me a switch, sir;" I answered, "Yes, sir," and off I went the third time, and brought one which I supposed would suit him. Then he said to me, "Come in here, sir." I answered, "Yes, sir." When I went into the stall, he told me to lie down, and I stooped down; he kicked me around for a while, then, making me lie on my face, he whipped me to his satisfaction.

That evening when I went home to father and mother, I said to them, "Mr. Young is whipping me too much now, I shall not stand it, I shall fight him." Father said to me, "You must not do that, because if you do he will say that your mother and I advised you to do it, and it will make it hard for your mother and me, as well as for yourself. You must do as I told you, my son: do your work the best you can, and do not say anything." I said to father, "But I don't know what I have done that he should whip me; he does not tell me what wrong I have done, he simply calls me to him and whips me when he gets ready." Father said, "I can do nothing more than to pray to the Lord to hasten the time when these things shall be done away; that is all I can do." When mother had stripped me and looked at the wounds that were upon me she burst into tears, and said, "If he were not so small I would not mind it so much; this will break his constitution; I am going to master about it, because I know he will not allow Mr. Young to treat this child so."

And I thought to myself that had mother gone to master about it, it would have helped me some, for he and she had grown up together and he thought a great deal of her. But father said to mother, "You better not go to master, for while he might stop the child from being treated badly, Mr. Young may revenge himself through the overseer, for you know that they are very friendly to each other." So said father to mother, "You would gain nothing in the end; the best thing for us to do is to pray much over it, for I believe that the time will come when this boy with the rest of the children will be free, though we may not live to see it."

When father spoke of liberty his words were of great comfort to me, and my heart swelled with the hope of a future, which made every moment seem an hour to me.

Father had a rule, which was strictly carried out as far as possible under the slave law, which was to put his children to bed early; but that night the whole family sat up late, while father and mother talked over the matter. It was a custom among the slaves not to allow their children under certain ages to enter into conversation with them; hence we could take no part with father and mother. As I was the object of their sympathy, I was allowed the privilege of answering the questions about the whipping the groom gave me.

When the time came for us to go to bed we all knelt down in family prayer, as was our custom; father's prayer seemed more real to me that night than ever before, especially in the words, "Lord, hasten the time when these children shall be their own free men and women."

My faith in father's prayer made me think that the Lord would answer him at the farthest in two or three weeks, but it was fully six years before it came, and father had been dead two years before the war.

After prayer we all went to bed; next morning father went to his work in the barn-yard, mother to hers in the field, and I to mine among the horses; before I started, however, father charged me carefully to keep his advice, as he said that would be the easiest way for me to get along.

But in spite of father's advice, I had made up my mind not to submit to the treatment of Mr. Young as before, seeing that it did not help me any. Things went smoothly for a while, until he called me to him, and ordered me to bring him a switch. I told him that I would bring him no more switches for him to whip me with, but that he must get them himself. After repeating the command very impatiently, and I refusing, he called to another boy named Hardy, who brought the switch, and then taking me into the stall he whipped me unmercifully.

After that he made me run back and forth every morning from a half to three quarters of an hour about two hundred and fifty yards, and every now and then he would run after me, and whip me to make me run faster. Besides that, when I was put upon a horse, if it threw me he would whip me, if it were five times a day. So I did not gain anything by refusing to bring switches for him to whip me with.

One very cold morning in the month of March, I came from home without washing my face, and Mr. Young made two of the slave boys take me down to a pond where the horses and mules used to drink; they threw me into the water and rubbed my face with sand until it bled, then I was made to run all the way to the stable, which was about a quarter of a mile. This cruel treatment soon hardened me so that I did not care for him at all.

A short time afterwards I was sent with the other boys about four or five miles from home, up the public road, to practice the horse, and they gave me a very wild animal to ride, which threw me very often. Mr. Young did not go with us, but sent a colored groom every morning, who was very faithful to every task alloted him; he was instructed to whip me every time the horse threw me while away from home. I got many little floggings by the colored groom, as the horse threw me, a great many times, but the floggings I got from him were very feeble compared with those of the white man; hence I was better content to go away with the colored groom than to be at home where I should have worse punishment.

But the time was coming when they ceased to whip me for being thrown by horses. One day, as I was riding along the road, the horse that I was upon darted at the sight of a bird, which flew across the way, throwing me upon a pile of brush. The horse stepped on my cheek, and the head of a nail in his shoe went through my left cheek and broke a tooth, but it was done so quickly that I hardly felt it. It happened that he did not step on me with his whole weight, if he had my jaw would have been broken. When I got up the colored groom was standing by me, but he could not whip me when he saw the blood flowing from my mouth, so he took me down to the creek, which was but a short distance from the place, and washed me, and then taking me home, sent for a doctor, who dressed the wound.

When Mr. Young saw my condition, he asked how it was done, and upon being told he said it ought to have killed me. After the doctor had dressed my face, of course I went home, thinking they would allow me to stay until I got well, but I had no sooner arrived than the groom sent for me; I did not answer, as my jaw pained me very much. When he found that I did not come, he came after me himself, and said if I did not come to the stable right away, he would whip me, so I went with him. He did not whip me while I was in that condition, but he would not let me lie down, so I suffered very much from exposure.

When mother came that night from the farm and saw my condition, she was overcome with grief; she said to father, "this wound is enough to kill the child, and that merciless man will not let him lie down until he gets well: this is too hard." Father said to her, "I know it is very hard, but what can we do? for if we try to keep this boy in the house it will cause us trouble." Mother said, "I wish they would take him out of the world, then he would be out of pain, and we should not have to fret about him, for he would be in heaven." Then she took hold of me and said, "Does it hurt you, son?" meaning my face, and I said, "Yes, mamma," and she shed tears; but she had no little toys to give me to comfort me; she could only promise me such as she had, which were eggs and chickens.

Father did not show his grief for me as mother did, but he tried to comfort mother all he could, and at times would say to me, "Never mind, my son, you will be a man bye and bye," but he did not know what was passing through my mind at that time. Though I was very small I thought that if, while a boy, my treatment was so severe, it would be much worse when I became a man, and having had a chance to see how men were being punished, it was a very poor consolation to me.

Finally the time came for us to go to bed, and we all knelt in family prayer. Father thanked God for having saved me from a worse injury, and then he prayed for mother's comfort, and also for the time which he predicted would come, that is, the time of freedom, when I and the rest of the children would be our own masters and mistresses; then he commended us to God, and we all went to bed. The next morning I went to my work with a great deal of pain. They did not send me up the road with the horses in that condition, but I had to ride the old horses to water, and work around the stable until I was well enough to go with the other boys. But I am happy to say that from the time I got hurt by that horse I was never thrown except through carelessness, neither was I afraid of a horse after that.

Notwithstanding father and mother fretted very much about me, they were proud of my success as a rider, but my hardships did not end here.

A short time after, I was taken to Columbia and Charleston, S.C., where they used to have the races. That year Col. Singleton won a large sum of money by the well-known horse, Capt. Miner, and that was the same season that I rode my trial race. The next year, before the time of racing, Col. Singleton died at his summer seat. After master's death, mistress sold all the race horses, and that put an end to sporting horses in that family.

I said that Boney Young, Col. Singleton's groom, had a brother by the name of Charles, who trained horses for the colonel's brother, John Singleton, Boney was a better trainer, but Charles was a better man to the negroes. It was against the law for a slave to buy spirituous liquors without a ticket, but Charles used to give the boys tickets to buy rum and whiskey with. He also allowed them to steal the neighbor's cows and hogs.

I remember that on one occasion his boys killed a cow belonging to a man by the name of Le Brun; soon after the meat was brought to the stable, Le Brun rode up on horseback with a loaded shot gun and threatened to shoot the party with whom the beef was found. Of course the negroes' apartments were searched; but as that had been anticipated, Mr. Young had made them put the meat in his apartment, and, as it was against the law of South Carolina for a white man to search another's house, or any apartment, without very strong evidence, the meat was not found. Before searching among the negroes, Mr. Young said to Le Brun, "You may search, but you won't find your beef here, for my boys don't steal." Le Brun answered, "Mr. Young, your word might be true, sir, but I would trust a nigger with money a great deal sooner than I would with cows and hogs." Mr. Young answered, "That might be true, but you won't find your beef here."

After their rooms and clothes had been searched, blood was found under some of their finger nails, which increased Le Brun's suspicion that they were of the party who stole his cow; but Mr. Young answered, "that blood is from rabbits my boys caught today." Mr. Le Brun tried to scare one of the boys, to make him say it was the blood of his cow. Mr. Young said, "Mr. Le Brun, you have searched and did not find your beef, as I told you that you would not; also I told you that the blood under their finger nails is from rabbits caught today. You will have to take my word, sir, without going to further trouble; furthermore, these boys belong to Mr. Singleton, and if you want to take further steps you will have to see him." Finding that he was not allowed to do as he wanted to, Mr. Le Brun made great oaths and threats as he mounted his horse to leave, that he would shoot the very first one of those boys he should catch near his cattle. He and Mr. Young never did agree after that.

But poor Mr. Young, as good as he was to the negroes, was an enemy to himself, for he was a very hard drinker. People who knew him before I did said they never had seen him drink tea, coffee, or water, but rather rum and whiskey; he drank so hard that he used to go into a crazy fit; he finally put an end to his life by cutting his throat with a razor, at a place called O'Handly's race course, about three miles from Columbia, S.C. This was done just a few days before one of the great races.

Boney Young drank, too, but not so hard as Charles. He lived until just after the late war, and, while walking one day through one of the streets of the above named city, dropped dead, with what was supposed to have been heart disease.

Boney had a mulatto woman, named Moriah, who had been originally brought from Virginia by negro traders, but had been sold to several different masters later. The trouble was that she was very beautiful, and wherever she was sold her mistresses became jealous of her, so that she changed owners very often. She was finally sold to Boney Young, who had no wife; and she lived with him until freed by the emancipation proclamation. She had two daughters; the elder's name was Annie, but we used to call her sissie; the younger's name was Josephine. Annie looked just like her father, Boney Young, while Josephine looked enough like Charles to have been his daughter. It was easy enough to tell that the mother had sprung from the negro race, but the girls could pass for white. Their mother, Moriah, died in Columbia some time after the war. Annie went off and was married to a white man, but I don't know what became of Josephine.

A short time before master's death he stood security for a northern man, who was cashier of one of the largest banks in the city of Charleston. This man ran away with a large sum of money, leaving the colonel embarassed, which fact made him very fretful and peevish. He had been none too good before to his slaves, and that made him worse, as you knew that the slave holders would revenge themselves on the slaves whenever they became angry. I had seen master whip his slaves a great many times, but never so severely as he did that spring before he died.

One day, before he went to his summer seat, he called a man to him, stripped and whipped him so that the blood ran from his body like water thrown upon him in cupfuls, and when the man stepped from the place where he had been tied, the blood ran out of his shoes. He said to the man, "You will remember me now, sir, as long as you live." The man answered, "Yes, master, I will."

Master went away that spring for the last time; he never returned alive; he died at his summer seat. When they brought his remains home all of the slaves were allowed to stop at home that day to see the last of him, and to lament with mistress. After all the slaves who cared to do so had seen his face, they gathered in groups around mistress to comfort her; they shed false tears, saying, "Never mind, missis, massa gone home to heaven." While some were saying this, others said, "Thank God, massa gone home to hell." Of course the most of them were glad that he was dead; but they were gathered there for the express purpose of comforting mistress. But after master's death mistress was a great deal worse than he had been.

When the master died there was a great change of things on the plantation; the creditors came in for settlement, so all of the fine horses, and some others, such as carriage horses, and a few mules also, were sold. The slaves whom master had bought himself had to be sold, but those who had been born on the plantation, given to him by his father, old Col. Dick Singleton, could not be sold until the grandchildren were of age.

As I have stated, my hardships and trials did not end with the race horses; you will now see them in another form.

After all the fine horses had been sold, mistress ordered the men and boys who were taking care of the horses to be put into the field, and I was among them, though small; but I had become so attached to the horses that they could get no work out of me, so they began to whip me, but every time they whipped me I would leave the field and run home to the barn-yard.

Finally mistress engaged a very bad man as overseer, in place of old Ben Usome, whose name was William Turner. Two or three days after his arrival he took me into the field and whipped me until I was sick, so I went home.

I went to mistress and told her that the overseer had whipped me; she asked if I had done the work that he had given me. I told her that master had promised me that, when I got too heavy to ride race horses, he would send me to learn the carpenter's trade; she asked me if, in case she put me to a trade, I would work, and I told her I would. So she consented.

But the overseer did not like the idea of having me work at the trade which was my choice. He said to mistress, "That is the worst thing you can do, madam, to allow a negro to have his choice about what he shall do. I have had some experience as an overseer for many years, and I think I am able to give a correct statement about the nature of negroes in general. I know a gentleman who allowed his negroes to have their own way about things on his plantation, and the result was that they got as high as their master. Besides that, madam, their influence rapidly spreads among the neighbors, and if such should be allowed, South Carolina would have all masters and mistresses, and no servants; and, as I have said, I know somewhat about the nature of negroes; I notice, madam, that this boy will put you to a great deal of trouble unless you begin to subdue him now while he is young. A very few years' delay will enable him to have a great influence among his fellow negroes, for that boy can read very well now, and you know, madam, it is against the law for a negro to get an education, and if you allow him to work at the carpenter's trade it will thus afford him the opportunity of acquiring a better education, because he will not be directly under the eye of one who will see that he makes no further advancement."

Then mistress asked me, "Can you read, Jacob?" I did not want her to know that I had taken notice of what they were saying, so I answered, "I don't know, ma'am." The overseer said, "He does not know what is meant, madam, but I can make him understand me." Then he took a newspaper from his pocket and said to me, "Can you say these words?" I took the paper and began to read, then he took it from me.

Mistress asked when I had learned to read and who had taught me. The overseer did not know, but said he would find out from me. Turning to me he took the paper from his pocket again, and said, "Jacob, who told you to say words in the book?" I answered, "Nobody, sir; I said them myself." He repeated the question three or four times, and I gave the same answer every time. Then mistress said, "I think it would be better to put him to trade than to have him in the field, because he will be away from his fellow-negroes, and will be less liable to influence them if we can manage to keep him away." The overseer said, "That might be true, madam, but if we can manage to keep him from gaining any more education he will eventually lose what little he has; and now, madam, if you will allow me to take him in hand, I will bring him out all right without injuring him." Just at this juncture a carriage drove up to the gate, and I ran as usual to open it, the overseer went about his business, and mistress went to speak to the persons in the carriage. I never had a chance to hear their conclusion.

A few days after the conversation between the overseer and mistress, I was informed by one of the slaves, who was a carpenter, that she had ordered that I should go to work at the trade with him. This gave me great joy, as I was very anxious to know what they had decided to do with me. I went to my new trade with great delight, and soon began to imagine what a famous carpenter I should make, and what I should say and do when I had learned the trade. Everything seemed to run smoothly with me for about two months, when suddenly I was told one morning that I must go into the field to drop cotton seed, but I did not heed the call, as mistress was not at home, and I knew she had just put me to the trade, also that the overseer was trying to get mistress' consent to have me work out in the field.

The next morning the overseer came into the carpenter's shop and said, "Did I not order ye into the field, sir?" I answered, "Yes, sir." "Well, why did ye not go?" I answered, "Mistress has put me here to learn the trade." He said, "I will give ye trade." So he stripped me and gave me a severe whipping, and told me that that was the kind of trade I needed, and said he would give me many of them. The next day I went into the field, and he put me to drop cotton seed, as I was too small to do anything else. I would have made further resistance, but mistress was very far away from home, and I had already learned the lesson that father and mother could render me no help, so I thought submission to him the easiest for me.

When I had got through with the cotton seed, in about three weeks, I went back to the carpenter's shop to work; so he came there and gave me another severe whipping, and said to me, "Ye want to learn the carpenter's trade, but I will have ye to the trade of the field." But that was the last whipping he gave me, and the last of his whip.

A few days after my last whipping the slaves were ordered down into the swamp across the river to clear up new grounds, while the already cleared lands were too wet from rain that had fallen that night. Of course I was among them to do my part; that is, while the men quartered up dry trees, which had been already felled in the winter, and rolled the logs together, the women, boys and girls piled the brushes on the logs and burned them.

We had to cross the river in a flat boat, which was too small to carry over all the slaves at once, so they had to make several trips.

Mr. Turner, the overseer, went across in the first flat; he did not ride down to the work place, but went on foot, while his horse, which was trained to stand alone without being hitched, was left at the landing place. My cousin and I crossed in the last boat. When we had got across we lingered behind the crowd at the landing; when they all were gone we went near the horse and saw the whip with which I was whipped a few days before fastened to the saddle. I said to him, "Here is the whip old Turner whipped me with the other day." He said, "It ought to be put where he will never get it to whip anybody with again." I answered my cousin, "If you will keep the secret I will put it where old Bill, as we used to call Mr. Turner, will never use it any more." He agreed to keep the secret, and then asked me how I would put the whip away. I told him if he would find me a string and a piece of iron I would show him how. He ran down to the swamp barn, which was a short distance from the margin of the river, and soon returned with the string and iron exactly suited for the work. I tied the iron to the whip, went into the flat boat, and threw it as far as I could into the river. My cousin and I watched it until it went out of sight under water; then, as guilty boys generally do after mischievous deeds, we dashed off in a run, hard as we could, among the other negroes, and acted as harmless as possible. Mr. Turner made several inquiries, but never learned what had become of his whip.

A short time after this, in the time of the war, in the year 1863, when a man was going round to the different plantations gathering slaves from their masters to carry off to work on fortifications and to wait on officers, there were ten slaves sent from Mrs. Singleton's plantation, and I was among them. They carried us to Sullivan's Island at Charleston, S.C., and I was there all of that year. I thanked God that it afforded me a better chance for an education than I had had at home, and so I was glad to be on the island. Though I had no one to teach me, as I was thrown among those of my fellow negroes who were fully as lame as I was in letters, yet I felt greatly relieved from being under the eye of the overseer, whose intention was to keep me from further advancement. The year after I had gone home I was sent back to Fort Sumpter--in the year 1864. I carried my spelling book with me, and, although the northerners were firing upon us, I tried to keep up my study.

In July of the same year I was wounded by the Union soldiers, on a Wednesday evening. I was taken to the city of Charleston, to Dr. Regg's hospital, and there I stayed until I got well enough to travel, when I was sent to Columbia, where I was when the hour of liberty was proclaimed to me, in 1865. This was the year of jubilee, the year which my father had spoken of in the dark days of slavery, when he and mother sat up late talking of it. He said to mother, "The time will come when this boy and the rest of the children will be their own masters and mistresses." He died six years before that day came, but mother is still enjoying liberty with her children.

And no doubt my readers would like to know how I was wounded in the war. We were obliged to do our work in the night, as they were firing on us in the day, and on a Wednesday night, just as we went out, we heard the cry of the watchman. "Look out." There was a little lime house near the southwest corner of the fort, and some twelve or thirteen of us ran into it, and all were killed but two; a shell came down on the lime house and burst, and a piece cut my face open. But as it was not my time to die, I lived to enjoy freedom.

I said that when I got so I could travel I was sent from Dr. Ragg's hospital in Charleston to Col. Singleton's plantation near Columbia, in the last part of the year 1864. I did not do any work during the remainder of that year, because I was unwell from my wound received in the fort.

About that time Gen. Sherman came through Georgia with his hundred thousand men, and camped at Columbia, S.C. The slave holders were very uneasy as to how they should save other valuables, as they saw that slavery was a hopeless case. Mistress had some of her horses, mules, cows and hogs carried down into the swamp, while the others which were left on the plantation were divided out to the negroes for safe keeping, as she had heard that the Yankees would not take anything belonging to the slaves. A little pig of about fifty or sixty pounds was given to me for safe keeping. A few of the old horses and mules were taken from the plantation by the Union soldiers, but they did not trouble anything else.

After Columbia had been burned, and things had somewhat quieted, along in the year 1865, the negroes were asked to give up the cows and hogs given them for safe keeping; all the rest gave up theirs, but mine was not found. No doubt but my readers want to know what had become of it. Well, I will tell you. You all know that Christmas was a great day with both masters and slaves in the South, but the Christmas of 1864 was the greatest which had ever come to the slaves, for, although the proclamation did not reach us until 1865, we felt that the chains which had bound us so long were well nigh broken.

So I killed the pig that Christmas, gathered all of my associates, and had a great feast, after which we danced the whole week. Mother would not let me have my feast in her cabin, because she was afraid that the white people would charge her with advising me to kill the pig, so I had it in one of the other slave's cabins.

When the overseer asked me for the pig given me, I told him that I killed it for my Christmas feast. Mistress said to me, "Jacob, why did you not ask me for the pig if you wanted it, rather than take it without permission?" I answered, "I would have asked, but thought, as I had it in hand, it wasn't any use asking for it." The overseer wanted to whip me for it, but as Uncle Sam had already broken the right arm of slavery, through the voice of the proclamation of 1863, he was powerless.

When the yoke had been taken from my neck I went to school in Columbia, S.C., awhile, then to Charleston. Afterward I came to Worcester, Mass., in February, 1869. I studied quite a while in the evening schools at Worcester, and also a while in the academy of the same place. During that time I was licensed a local preacher of the African Methodist Episcopal church, and sometime later was ordained deacon at Newport, RI.

A short time after my ordination I was sent to Salem, Mass., where I have remained, carrying on religious work among my people, trying in my feeble way to preach that gospel which our blessed Saviour intended for the redemption of all mankind, when he proclaimed, "Go ye into all the world and preach the gospel." In the meantime I have been striking steady blows for the improvement of my education, in preparing myself for a field of work among my more unfortunate brethren in the South.

I must say that I have been surrounded by many good friends, including the clergy, since I have been in Salem, whose aid has enabled me to serve a short term in the Wesleyan school at Wilbraham, Mass., also to begin a course of theological studies at Talladega college in Alabama, which I am endeavoring to complete by the sale of this publication.

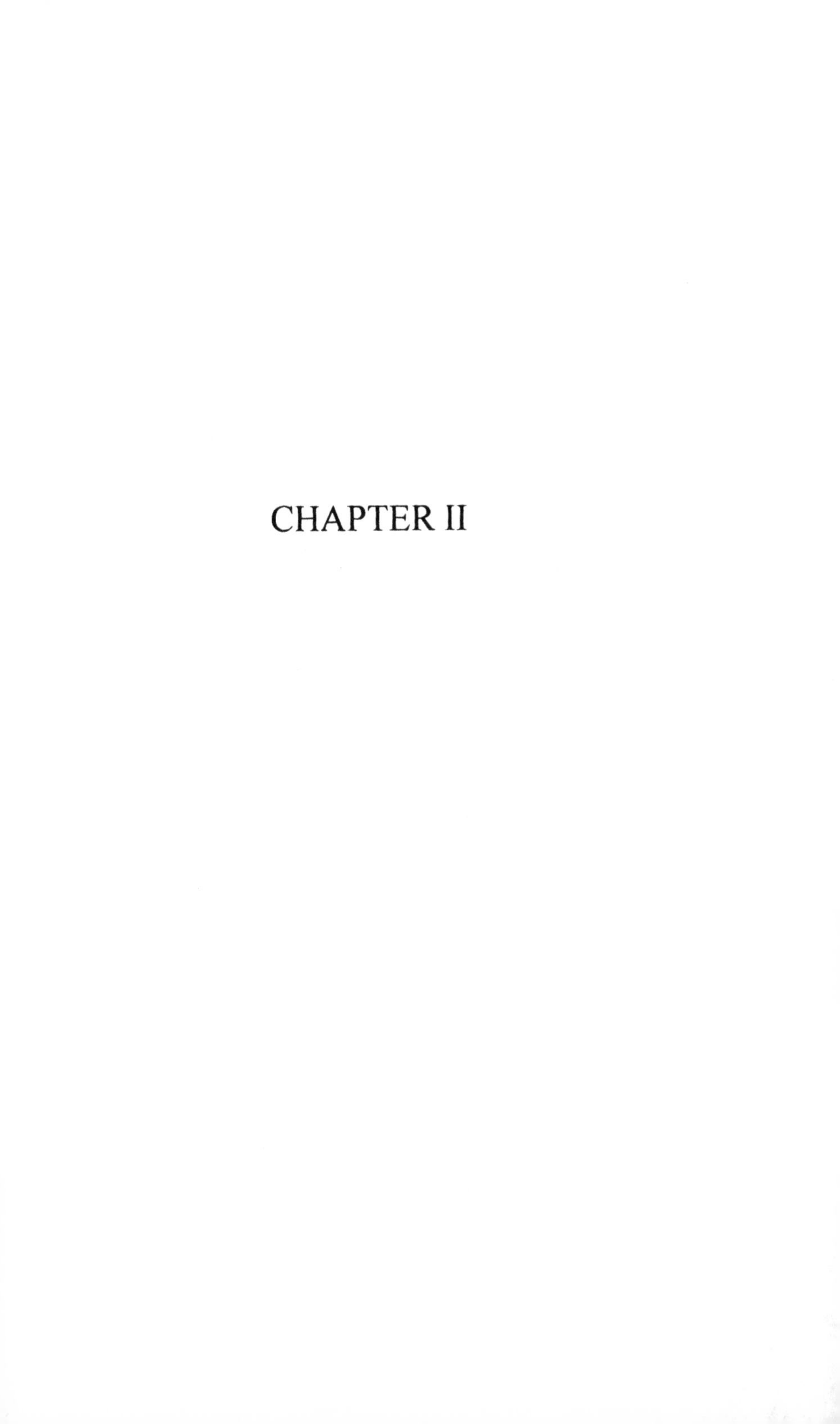

CHAPTER II

CHAPTER II.--SKETCHES.

THE SALE OF MY TWO SISTERS.

I have stated that my father had fifteen children--four boys and three girls by his first wife, and six boys and two girls by his second. Their names are as follows: Toney, Azerine, Duke and Dezine, of the girls, Violet, Priscilla and Lydia; those of the second wife as follows: Footy, Embrus, Caleb, Mitchell, Cuffee, and Jacob, who is the author, and the girls, Catherine and Retta.

As I have said, old Col. Dick Singleton had two sons and two daughters, and each had a plantation. Their names were John, Matt, Marianna and Angelico. They were very agreeable together, so that if one wanted negro help from another's plantation, he or she could have it, especially in cotton picking time.

John Singleton had a place about twenty miles from master's, and master used to send him slaves to pick cotton. At one time my master, Col. M.R. Singleton, sent my two sisters, Violet and Priscilla, to his brother John, and while they were there they married two of the men on his place. By mutual consent master allowed them to remain on his brother's place. But some time after this John Singleton had some of his property destroyed by water, as is often the case in the South at the time of May freshets, what is known in the North as high tides.

One of these freshets swept away John Singleton's slave houses, his barns, with horses, mules and cows. These caused his death by a broken heart, and since he owed a great deal of money his slaves had to be sold. A Mr. Manning bought a portion of them, and Charles Login the rest. These two men were known as the greatest slave traders in the South. My sisters were among the number that Mr. Manning bought.

He was to take them into the state of Louisiana for sale, but some of the men did not want to go with him, and he put those in prison until he was ready to start. My sisters' husbands were among the prisoners in the Sumterville jail, which was about twenty-five or thirty miles across the river from master's place. Those who did not show any unwillingness to go were allowed to visit their relatives and friends for the last time. So my sisters, with the rest of their unfortunate companions, came to master's place to visit us. When the day came for them to leave, some, who seemed to have been willing to go at first, refused, and were handcuffed together and guarded on their way to the cars by white men. The women and children were driven to the depot in crowds, like so many cattle, and the sight of them caused great excitement among master's negroes. Imagine a mass of uneducated people shedding tears and yelling at the top of their voices in anguish.

The victims were to take the cars at a station called Clarkson turnout, which was about four miles from master's place. The excitement was so great that the overseer and driver could not control the relatives and friends of those that were going away, as a large crowd of both old and young went down to the depot to see them off. Louisiana was considered by the slaves a place of slaughter, so those who were going did not expect to see their friends again. While passing along many of the negroes left their masters' fields and joined us as we marched to the cars; some were yelling and wringing their hands, while others were singing little hymns that they had been accustomed to for the consolation of those that were going away, such as

"When we all meet in heaven,
There is no parting there;
When we all meet in heaven,
There is parting no more."

We arrived at the depot and had to wait for the cars to bring the others from the Sumterville jail, but they soon came in sight, and when the noise of the cars had died away, we heard wailing and shrieks from those in the cars. While some were weeping, others were fiddling, picking banjo, and dancing as they used to do in their cabins on the plantations. Those who were so merry had very bad masters, and even though they stood a chance of being sold to one as bad or even worse, yet they were glad to be rid of the one they knew.

While the cars were at the depot a large crowd of white people gathered, laughing and talking about the prospect of negro traffic; but when the cars began to start, and the conductor cried out, "All who are going on this train must get on board without delay," the colored people cried out with one voice as though the heavens and earth were coming together, and it was so pitiful that those hard-hearted white men, who had been accustomed to driving slaves all their lives, shed tears like children. As the cars moved away we heard the weeping and wailing from the slaves as far as human voice could be heard; and from that time to the present I have neither seen nor heard from my two sisters, nor any of those who left Clarkson depot on that memorable day.

THE WAY THE SLAVES LIVED.

Most of the cabins in the time of slavery were built so as to contain two families; some had partitions, while others had none. When there were no partitions each family would fit up its own part as it could; sometimes they got old boards and nailed them up, stuffing the cracks with rags; when they could not get boards they hung up old clothes. When the family increased the children all slept together, both boys and girls, until one got married; then a part of another cabin was assigned to that one, but the rest would have to remain with their mother and father, as in childhood, unless they could get with some of their relatives or friends who had small families, or unless they were sold; but of course the rules of modesty were held in some degrees by the slaves, while it could not be expected that they could entertain the highest degree of it, on account of their condition. A portion of the time the young men slept in the apartment known as the kitchen, and the young women slept in the room with their mother and father. The two families had to use one fireplace. One who was accustomed to the way in which the slaves lived in their cabins could tell as soon as they entered whether they were friendly or not, for when they did not agree the fires of the two families did not meet on the hearth, but there was a vacancy between them, that was a sign of disagreement. In a case of this kind, when either of the families stole a hog, cow or sheep from the master, he had to carry it to some of his friends, for fear of being betrayed by the other family. On one occasion a man, who lived with one unfriendly, stole a hog, killed it, and carried some of the meat home. He was seen by some one of the other family, who reported him to the overseer, and he gave the man a severe whipping. Sometime afterward this man who had been betrayed thought he would get even with his enemy; so about two months later he killed another hog, and, after eating a part of it, stole into the apartment of the other family and hid a portion of the meat among the old clothes. Then he told the overseer that he had seen the man go out late that night and that he had not come home until the next morning; when he did come he had called his wife to the window and she had taken something in. He did not know what it was, but if the overseer would go there right away he would find it. The overseer went and searched and found the meat, so the man was whipped. He told the overseer that the other man put it in his apartment while the family were away, but the overseer told him that every man must be responsible for his own apartment.

No doubt you would like to know how the slaves could sleep in their cabins in summer, when it was so very warm. When it was too warm for them to sleep comfortably, they all slept under trees until it grew too cool, that is along in the month of October. Then they took up their beds and walked.

JOE AND THE TURKEY.

Joe was a boy who was waiter to his master, one Mr. King, and he and his wife were very fond of company. Mrs. King always had chickens and turkey for dinner, but at one time the company was so large that they did not leave anything for the servants; so that day, finding that all had been eaten, while mistress and master were busy with the company, Joe killed a turkey, dressed it and put it into the pot, but, as he did not cut it up, the turkey's knees stuck out of the pot, and, as he could not cover them up, he put one of his shirts over them. When Mrs. King called Joe, he answered, but did not go right away as he generally did, and when he did go his mistress said, "Joe, what was the matter with you?" he answered, "Noffing, missis." Then he went and opened the gate for the company. Soon after, Joe was back in the kitchen again, and Mrs. King went down to see what he was doing; seeing the pot on she said, "Joe, what is in that pot?" he said, "noffing, missis, but my shirt; am gwine to wash it." She did not believe him, so she took a fork and stuck it in the pot, taking out the shirt, and she found the turkey. She asked him how the turkey had got into the pot; he said he did not know but reckoned the turkey got in himself, as the fowls were very fond of going into the kitchen. So Joe was whipped because he allowed the turkey to get into the pot.

THE CUSTOM OF CHRISTMAS.

Both masters and slaves regarded Christmas as a great day. When the slaveholders had made a large crop they were pleased, and gave the slaves from five to six days, which were much enjoyed by the negroes, especially by those who could dance. Christmas morning was held sacred both by master and slaves, but in the afternoon, or in a part of the next day the slaves were required to devote themselves to the pleasure of their masters. Some of the masters would buy presents for the slaves, such as hats and tobacco for the men, handkerchiefs and little things for the women; these things were given after they had been pleased with them; after either dancing or something for their amusement.

When the slaves came up to their masters and mistresses, the latter would welcome them, the men would take off their hats and bow and the women would make a low courtesy. There would be two or three large pails filled with sweetened water, with a gallon or two of whiskey in each; this was dealt out to them until they were partly drunk; while this was going on, those who could talk very well would give tokens of well wishing to their master and mistress, and some who were born in Africa, would sing some of their songs, or tell different stories of the customs in Africa. After this they would spend half a day in dancing in some large cotton house or on a scaffold, the master providing fiddlers who came from other plantations if there were none on the place, and who received from fifteen to twenty dollars on these occasions.

A great many of the strict members of the church who did not dance would be forced to do it to please their masters; the favorite tunes were "The Fisher's Hornpipe," "The Devil's Dream," and "Black-eyed Susan." No one can describe the intense emotion in the negro's soul on those occasions when they were trying to please their masters and mistresses.

After the dancing was over we had our presents, master giving to the men, and mistress to the women; then the slaves would go to their quarters and continue to dance the rest of the five or six days, and would sometimes dance until eight o'clock Sunday morning. The cabins were mostly made of logs, and there were large cracks in them so that a person could see the light in them for miles in the night, and of course the sun's rays would shine through them in the daytime, so on Sunday morning when they were dancing and did not want to stop you would see them filling up the cracks with old rags. The idea was that it would not be Sunday inside if they kept the sun out, and thus they would not desecrate the Sabbath; and these things continued until the freedom of the slaves.

Perhaps my readers would like to know if most of the negroes were inclined to violate the Sabbath. They were; as the masters would make them do unnecessary work, they got into the habit of disregarding the day as one for rest, and did many things Sunday that would not be allowed in the North. At that time, if you should go through the South on those large cotton and rice plantations, while you would find some dancing on Sunday, others would be in the woods and fields hunting rabbits and other game, and some would be killing pigs belonging to their masters or neighbors. I remember when a small boy I went into the woods one Sunday morning with one of my fellow negroes whose name was Munson, but we called him Pash, and we killed one of master's pigs, hid it under the leaves until night, then took it home and dressed it. That was the only time I killed a pig, but I knew of thousands of cases like this in the time of slavery. But thank God, the year of Jubilee has come, and the negroes can return from dancing, from hunting, and from the master's pig pens on Sundays and become observers of the Sabbath, of good moral habits and men of equal rights before the law.

PUNISHMENTS INFLICTED ON DIFFERENT ONES.

One of my fellow negroes, who belonged to Col. M.R. Singleton, visited the plantation of the Col.'s sister; the overseer of that plantation had forbidden strangers to go there, but this man, whose name was Harry, would go. The overseer heard of him but could not catch him, but the overseer of master's place sent him to Mr. Jackson (the overseer of master's sister's place). Mr. Jackson tied him and hit him three hundred lashes and then said to him, "Harry, if you were not such a good nigger I should have given you a first class whipping, but as you are a good fellow, and I like you so well, I thought I would give you a light flogging now; you must be a good nigger and behave yourself, for if I ever have to take hold of you again, I shall give you a good whipping." When Mr. Jackson had loosed him from where he had tied him, Harry was so exhausted that he fell down, so Mr. Jackson sent him home in a cart, and he had to stay at home from work a month or two, and was never the same man again.

THE PUNISHMENT AND SALE OF MONDAY.

There was a man who belonged to master by the name of Monday, who was a good field hand; in summer the tasks generally performed by the slaves were more than they could do, and in consequence they were severely whipped, but Monday would not wait to be whipped, but would run away before the overseer or driver could get to him. Sometimes master would hire a white man who did nothing else but hunt runaway slaves for a living; this man would take from fifteen to twenty hounds with him to hunt Monday, but often he would be out three or four months; when he was caught and brought home, he was put in prison and was whipped every day for a week or two, but just as soon as he could he would run away again.

At one time when he had been brought home, one of his arms was tied and he was put in care of a keeper who made him work with the other slaves, days, and put him in confinement nights, but for all this he got away from his keeper and went into the woods again. The last time he ran away two white men were hired to hunt him; they had about twenty-five blood hounds, but this time Monday fell in with another slave who had ran away from his master and had been in the woods seven years, and they together were able to kill a greater portion of the hounds. Finally the white men caught his companion, but did not catch Monday, though they chased him two or three days longer, but he came home himself; they did not whip him and he went to work in the field. Things went on very nicely with him for two or three weeks, until one day a white man was seen riding through the fields with the overseer; of course the slaves did not mistrust his object, as white men often visited master's plantation, but that night, when all the slaves were sleeping, the man that was seen in the daytime went to the door of Monday's cabin and called him out of his bed, and when he had come to his door, the stranger, whom he had never seen before that day, handcuffed him and said, "You now belong to me." Most of the slaves found it out, as Monday was put in a cart and carried through the streets of the negro quarters, and there was quite an excitement, but Monday was never heard from again.

THE STORY OF JAMES HAY.

There was a slave named James Hay, who belonged to a neighbor of master's; he was punished a great many times because he could not get his task done. The other slaves pitied him because he seemed unable to perform his task. One evening he got a severe whipping; the next morning as the slaves were having their tasks assigned them, an old lady by the name of Aunt Patience went by, and said, "Never mind, Jim, my son, the Lord will help you with your task today;" he answered, "Yes, ma'am." He began his work very faithfully and continued until it was half done, then he lay down under a tree; the others, not understanding his motive, thought he was tired and was taking a rest, but he did not return to his task until the overseer called him and asked him why he did not have his work nearer done. He said, "Aunt Patience told me dis morning that the Lord would help me today, and I thought as I did half of the task, the Lord might have finished the other half if he intended to help me at all." The overseer said "You see that the Lord did not come to help you and we shall not wait for him, but we will help you;" so Jim got a severe punishment. Sometime after this, Jim Hay was called upon by some professors of religion; they asked him if he was not tired of serving the devil, and told him that the Lord was good and had helped many of his people, and would help all who asked him and then take them home to heaven. Jim said that if the Lord would not do half an acre of his task for him when he depended on him, he did not think he could trust him, and Jim never became a Christian to my knowledge.

THE STORY OF MR. USOM AND JACK.

One Sunday when the boys were at the overseer's, Mr. Usom's house, as we generally were, he said to one, "Jack, don't you think that hell is a very hot place, if it is as they describe it?" Jack said, "Yes, massa." Mr. Usom said, "Well, how do you think it will be with poor fellows that have to go there?" "Well, Massa Bob, I will tell you what I tinks about it, I tinks us niggers need not trouble usselves about hell, as the white folks." "How is that, Jack?" Jack answered, "Because us niggers have to work out in the hot sun, and if we go to hell it would not be so bad for us because us used to heat, but it will be bad for white folks because they is not used to hot weather."

THE STORY OF JAMES SWINE AND HIS DEATH.

There was a negro who belonged to one Mr. Clarkson; he was called Jim Swine; his right name was James, but he was called Jim Swine because he loved hog meat and would often steal hogs from his master or from the neighbors; he was a very able-bodied man, weighing about two hundred and twenty-five pounds, and a very good field hand. Of course it is generally known that a great many of the slaves were poorly fed, so it was natural that they should take anything they could to sustain life. As his master had only a few hogs, he stole many from the neighbors and was punished a great many times for it.

Sometimes he was punished when a hog was missing, even though they did not find the meat with him. Jim was not in the habit of running away much, but if they whipped him when he had not stolen the hog they accused him of taking, he would go away into the woods and stay until he got ready to come home. He was so strong that they were afraid of him; three or four men would not attack him when in the woods. The last time Jim stole hogs he was caught in the act of taking one from my master, Col. Singleton. They tied him, and Mr. Clarkson's overseer was sent for, who was his own son, Thomas Clarkson. Jim was taken home, whipped, and a cured middling of a hog was tied around his neck; he was then made to work along with the other slaves in the day and was put in prison in the night for two weeks. One morning when the overseer went to his place of confinement to take him into the field, he found him dead, with a large piece of meat hanging to his neck. The news of his death soon went abroad, also the cause of it, and when old Mr. Clarkson found it out he was very angry at his son Thomas, and his punishment was, that he was driven from his plantation with orders never to return, and that he should not have any of his property. This seemed to grieve Thomas very much, and he made several attempts to regain his father's affections, but failed. Finally, one night, Thomas made an outcry that he had found a pearl of great price, that the Lord had pardoned his sins, and that he was at peace with all mankind. When his father heard of this, he sent for him to come home, and he gave him quite a sum of money and willed him the portion of property that he had said he should keep from him. But poor Jim was not there to forgive him.

A MAN MISTAKEN FOR A HOG.

Two negroes went to steal hogs from their masters. The swine were under a barn, as in the South barns were made high enough for hogs to stand under. The man who went under the barn said to the other, you must strike the hog that goes the slowest; then he went under the barn on his knees to drive them out while the other stood with his club ready to strike, but they ran out so fast he could not hit them, except the last as he thought, which came just slow enough, and he struck. While the supposed hog was kicking, he jumped upon it to stab it with his knife but found it was his companion.

CUSTOM OF WITCHES AMONG SLAVES.

The witches among slaves were supposed to have been persons who worked with them every day, and were called old hags or jack lanterns. Those, both men and women, who, when they had grown old looked old, were supposed to be witches. Sometimes, after eating supper, the negroes would gather in each other's cabins which looked over the large openings on the plantation, and when they would see a light at a great distance and see it open and shut, they would say, "there is an old hag," and if it came from a direction in which those lived whom they called witches, one would say, "Dat looks like old Aunt Susan;" another would say, "No, dat look like man hag;" still another, "I tink dat look like ole Uncle Renty."

When the light had disappeared they said that the witch had got into the plantation and changed itself into a person and had gone about on the place talking with the people like others until those whom it wanted to bewitch went to bed, then it would change itself to a witch again. They claimed that the witches rode human beings like horses, and that the spittle that ran on the side of the cheek when one slept, was the bridle that the witch rode with. Sometimes a baby would be smothered by its mother, and they would charge it to a witch. If they went out hunting at night and were lost, it was believed that a witch had led them off, especially if they fell into a pond or creek. I was very much troubled with witches when a little boy and am now sometimes, but it is only when I eat a hearty supper and immediately go to bed. It was said by some of the slaves that the witches would sometimes go into the rooms of the cabins and hide themselves until the family went to bed and therefore when any one claimed that he had gone into the apartment before bed time and thought he had seen a witch, if he had an old Bible in the cabin, that would be taken into the room, and the person who carried the Bible would say as he went in, "In de name of de Fader and of de Son and de Holy Gos wat you want?" Then the Bible would be put in the corner where the person thought he had seen the witch, as it was generally believed that if this were done the witch could not stay. When they could not get the Bible they used red pepper and salt pounded together and scattered in the room, but in this case they generally felt the effects of it more than the witch, for when they went to bed it made them cough all night. When I was a little boy my mother sent me into the cabin room for something, and as I got in I saw something black and white, but did not stop to see what it was, and running out said there was a witch in the room. But father, having been born in Africa, did not believe in such things, so he called me a fool and whipped me and the witch got scared and ran out the door. It turned out to be our own black and white cat that we children played with every day. Although it proved to be the cat, and father did not believe in witches, still I held the idea that there were such things, for I thought the majority of the people believed it, and that they ought to know more than could one man. Sometime after I was free, in travelling from Columbia to Camden, a distance of about thirty-two miles, night overtook me when about half way there; it was very dark and rainy, and as I approached a creek I saw a great number of lights of those witches opening and shutting. I did not know what to do and thought of turning back, but when I looked behind I saw some witches in the distance, so I said, "If I turn back those will meet me and I shall be in as much danger as if I go on", and I thought of what some of my fellow negroes had said about their leading men into ponds and creeks. There was a creek just ahead, so I concluded that I should be drowned that night; however, I went on, as I saw no chance of turning back. When I came near the creek one of the witches flew into my face. I jumped back and grasped it, but it proved to be one of those lightning bugs, and I thought that if all the witches were like that one, I should not be in any great danger from them.

THE DEATH OF CYRUS AND STEPNEY.

Old Col. Dick Singleton had several state places as I have mentioned. In the South, the rich men who had a great deal of money bought all the plantations they could get and obtained them very cheap. The Colonel had some ten or twenty places and had slaves settled on each of them.

He had four children, and after each had received a plantation, the rest were called state places, and these could not be sold until all the grandchildren should become of age; after they all had received places, the rest could be sold.

One of the places was called Biglake. The slaves on these places were treated more cruelly than on those where the owner lived, for the overseers had full sway.

One day the overseer at Biglake punished the slaves so that some of them fell exhausted. When he came to the two men, Cyrus and Stepney, they resisted, but were taken by force and severely punished. A few days afterwards the overseer died, and those two men were taken up and hanged on the plantation without judge or jury.

After that another overseer was hired, with orders to arm himself, and every slave who did not submit to his punishment was to be shot immediately. At times, when the overseer was angry with a man he would strike him on the head with a club and kill him instantly, and they would bury him in the field. Some would run away and come to M.R. Singleton, my master, but he would only tell them to go home and behave. Then they were handcuffed or chained and carried back to Biglake, and when we would hear from them again the greater part would have been murdered. When they were taken from master's place, they would bid us good bye and say they knew they should be killed when they got home.

Oh! who can paint the sad feeling in our minds when we saw these, our own race, chained and carried home to drink the bitter cup of death from their merciless oppressors, with no one near to say, "Spare him, God made him," or to say, "Have mercy on him, for Jesus died for him." His companions dared not groan above a whisper for fear of sharing the same fate; but thanks that the voice of the Lord was heard in the North, which said, "Go quickly to the South and let my prison-bound people go free, for I have heard their cries from cotton, corn and rice plantations, saying, how long before thou wilt come to deliver us from this chain?" and the Lord said to them, "Wait, I will send you John Brown who shall be the key to the door of your liberty, and I will harden the heart of Jefferson Davis, your devil, that I may show him and his followers my power; then shall I send you Abraham Lincoln, mine angel, who shall lead you from the land of bondage to the land of liberty." Our fathers all died in "the wilderness," but thank God, the children reached "the promised land."

THE WAY THE SLAVES DETECTED THIEVES AMONG THEMSELVES

The slaves had three ways of detecting thieves, one with a Bible, one with a sieve, and another with graveyard dust. The first way was this:--four men were selected, one of whom had a Bible with a string attached, and each man had his own part to perform. Of course this was done in the night as it was the only time they could attend to such matters as concerned themselves. These four would commence at the first cabin with every man of the family, and one who held the string attached to the Bible would say, "John or Tom," whatever the person's name was, "you are accused of stealing a chicken or a dress from Sam at such a time," then one of the other two would say, "John stole the chicken," and another would say, "John did not steal the chicken." They would continue their assertions for at least five minutes, then the man would put a stick in the loop of the string that was attached to the Bible, and holding it as still as he could, one would say, "Bible, in the name of the Father and of the Son and of the Holy Ghost, if John stole that chicken, turn," that is, if the man had stolen what he was accused of, the Bible was to turn around on the string, and that would be a proof that he did steal it. This was repeated three times before they left that cabin, and it would take those men a month sometimes when the plantation was very large, that is if they did not find the right person before they got through the whole place.

The second way they had of detecting thieves was very much like the first, only they used a sieve instead of a Bible; they stuck a pair of scissors in the sieve with a string hitched to it and a stick put through the loop of the string and the same words were used as for the Bible. Sometimes the Bible and the sieve would turn upon the names of persons whose characters were beyond suspicion. When this was the case they would either charge the mistake to the men who fixed the Bible and the sieve, or else the man who was accused by the turning of the Bible and the sieve, would say that he passed near the coop from which the fowl was stolen, then they would say, "Bro. John we see dis how dat ting work, you pass by de chicken coop de same night de hen went away."

But when the Bible or the sieve turned on the name of one whom they knew often stole, and he did not acknowledge that he had stolen the chicken of which he was accused, he would have to acknowledge his previously stolen goods or that he had thought of stealing at the time when the chicken or the dress was stolen. Then this examining committee would justify the turning of the Bible or sieve on the above statement of the accused person.

The third way of detecting thieves was taught by the fathers and mothers of the slaves. They said no matter how untrue a man might have been during his life, when he came to die he had to tell the truth and had to own everything he had ever done, and whatever dealing those alive had with anything pertaining to the dead, must be true, or they would immediately die and go to hell to burn in fire and brimstone. So in consequence of this, the graveyard dust was the truest of the three ways in detecting thieves. The dust would be taken from the grave of a person who had died last and put into a bottle with water. Then two of the men of the examining committee would use the same words as in the case of the Bible and the sieve, "John stole that chicken," "John did not steal that chicken," and after this had gone on for about five minutes, then one of the other two who attended to the Bible and the sieve would say, "John, you are accused of stealing that chicken that was taken from Sam's chicken coop at such a time." "In the name of the Father and the Son and the Holy Ghost, if you have taken Sam's chicken don't drink this water, for if you do you will die and go to hell and be burned in fire and brimstone, but if you have not you may take it and it will not hurt you." So if John had taken the chicken he would own it rather than take the water.

Sometimes those whose characters were beyond suspicion would be proven thieves when they tried the graveyard dust and water. When the right person was detected, if he had any chickens he had to give four for one, and if he had none he made it good by promising that he would do so no more. If all the men on the plantation passed through the examination and no one was found guilty, the stolen goods would be charged to strangers. Of course these customs were among the negroes for their own benefit, for they did not consider it stealing when they took anything from their master.

JOSH AND THE CORN.

A man engaged in stripping fodder put some green ears of corn in the fire to roast as the slaves generally do in fodder stripping time, although they were whipped when caught. Before the ears were roasted enough, the overseer approached, and Josh took the ears out with some live coals stuck to them and put them in his shirt bosom. In running away his clothes took fire and Josh jumped into a creek to put it out. The overseer said to him, "Josh, what are you doing there?" He answered, "It is so warm today I taught I would go in de creek to git cool off, sir." "Well, have you got cooled off, Josh?" "Oh! yes, sir, very much cooler, sir."

Josh was a very hearty eater, so that the peck of corn flour allowed the slaves for a week's ration lasted him only a half. He used to lug large sticks of wood on his shoulders from the woods, which was from a mile to a mile and a half away, to first one and then another of his fellow negroes, who gave him something to eat; and in that way he made out his week's rations.

His habit was to bring the wood at night, throw it down at the cabin door, and, as he walked in, some one of the family would say, "Well, Josh, you fetched us a piece of wood." He would burst into one of his jolly laughs and answer, "Yes." Soon after they had given him something to eat, Josh would bid them good night, but when he went, the wood disappeared too. He would throw it down at another cabin door as before, go in and get something to eat; but every time when he went away the wood would be missing until he had found enough to eat, when he would leave it at the last cabin. Those to whom Josh carried the wood accused others of stealing it, and when they asked him about it, he only laughed and said that the wood was at the door when he came out.

Josh continued the trick for quite a while. Finally one night he brought a stick of wood and threw it down at a cabin door, walked in and got something to eat as usual. But as he came in, the man of the family, to whom he carried the wood, bade him good night, and said that he had business out which would keep him so late, that Josh would be gone before he got back. While Josh was busy laughing and talking with the rest of the family the man went out, and secreted himself in the chimney corner of another cabin, and it was not long after he took his stand before Josh bade the family good night, came out whistling, and shouldered the wood, but as he started off the watchman cried out, "Is that you, Josh?" Josh threw the wood down and answered, "O no, tisn't me." Of course Josh was so funny one couldn't get angry with him if he wanted to; but the rest of the slaves found out after that how the wood Josh brought them, was missing.

But poor Josh died at last, away from home; he was sent with some of the other negroes from Mrs. M.R. Singleton's plantation at Columbia, in the year 1864, to build fortifications as a defence, under Gen. Wade Hampton against Gen. Sherman, and while there he was taken sick and died, under the yoke of slavery, having heard of freedom but not living to enjoy it.

RUNAWAY SLAVES.

My readers, have, no doubt, already heard that there were men in the South who made it their business in the days of slavery to raise and train hounds especially to hunt slaves with. Most of the owners hired such men on condition that they were to capture and return their runaway slaves, without being bruised and torn by the dogs. The average sums paid hunters were ten, fifteen and twenty-five dollars for capturing a slave; very many times, these sums were taken from the overseer's salary, as they were more or less the cause of slaves running away.

My readers want to know whether the runaway slaves ever returned to the overseers and their masters without being caught by the hunters. Sometimes they did and sometimes they never returned. Some stayed their lifetime; others, who would have returned, fell sick and died in the woods.

My readers ask, how did the slaves at home know when their fellow negroes, the runaways, sickened or died in the woods. In general, some one on the plantation from which they ran away, or confidential friends on some other plantation, had communication with them, so that if anything happened to them the slaves at home would find out through such parties. And sometimes the masters and overseers would find out about their death, but indirectly, however, because if it was known that any one on the plantation had dealings with the runaway, he would be punished, even though the information should be gladly received by the master and overseer.

Sometimes groups of runaway slaves, of eight, ten and even twenty, belonging to different owners, got together in the woods, which made it very difficult and dangerous for slave hunters to capture those whom they were hired to hunt. In such cases sometimes these runaways killed both hunters and dogs. The thick forests in which they lived could not be searched on horseback, neither could man or dog run in them. The only chances the hunters had of catching runaway slaves were either to rout them from those thick forests or attack them when they came out in the opening to seek food.

Of course the runaways were mostly armed, and when attacked in the forests they would fight. My readers ask, how had they obtained arms and what were those arms, since slaves were not allowed to have deadly weapons? Some had large knives made by their fellow negroes who were blacksmiths, others stole guns from white men who were accustomed to lay them carelessly around when they were out hunting game. The runaways who stole the guns were kept in powder and shot by some of the other slaves at home, who bought such from poor white men who kept little country stores in the different parts of the South.

The runaway slaves generally had fathers, brothers, cousins, or confidential friends who met them at certain appointed places, and brought them such things as were needed. The most they wanted from their fellow negroes at home was salt and a little corn flour; for they lived principally on beef and swine meat, taken either from their own masters or some other's stock.

My readers ask, did not some of the slaves at home betray their fellow negroes, the runaways, to the white man? I answer, they did; but often such were well spotted, and if the runaway slaves got a chance at them while in the woods would mob or kill them. On the other hand when they met those whom they could trust, instead of injuring them, they exchanged beef and swine meat with them for bread, corn flour, and salt, such as they needed in the woods.

THE RUNAWAY SLAVES IN THE HOUSE.

Instead of going into the woods, sometimes runaway slaves lived right around the overseer's and master's houses for months. A slave, named Isom, ran away from Thomas Clarkson, his master's son, who was the overseer. Mr. Clarkson was satisfied, as he said, that the unaccustomed runaway, whom he thought was in the woods could not stay from home long, but finding that he stayed longer than expected, Mr. Clarkson hired a slave hunter with his dogs to hunt him.

The hunter came early to the plantation and took breakfast with Mr. Clarkson on the day they began to hunt for the runaway slave. While sitting at breakfast, Mr. Clarkson said to the hunter, "My father brought up that boy as a house servant, and petted him so that it takes all the salt in the country to cure him. Father had too much religion to keep his negroes straight; but I don't believe in that. I think a negro ought to be overhauled every little while to keep him in his place, and that is just the reason why I took the overseership on this plantation."

The Hunter. "Well, what caused your boy to run away, Mr. Clarkson?"

Mr. Clarkson. "Well he ran away because I gave him an overhauling, to keep him in the place of a negro."

Mr. Clarkson's wife. "Well, Thomas, I told you the other day, before you did it, that I didn't see any need of your whipping Isom, because I thought he was a good boy."

Mr. Clarkson. "Yes, my dear, if South Carolina had many more such Presbyterians as you and Father Boston (he meant old Mr. Clarkson), in a short time there would be no slaves in the state; then who would you have to work for you?"

I wish to state a fact to my readers. While there were exceptions, as a general thing the Presbyterians made better masters than did any other denomination among the slave holders in the South.

Mrs. Clarkson. "Yes, Thomas, if you were such a Presbyterian as you charged Father Boston and me with being, you could have saved yourself the trouble and money which it will cost to hunt him."

Mr. Clarkson. "Well, we will not discuss the matter of religion any further." (To the hunter.) "That boy has been away now for several days since I whipped him. I thought that he would have returned home long before this time, as this is the first time he has ever run away; but I rather conclude that he got with some experienced runaways. Now do you think that you can capture him without his being hurt, or torn by your dogs?"

Mrs. Clarkson. "That is just what I am afraid will be done to that boy."

The Hunter. "O, no fear of that, madam, I shall use care in hunting him. I have but one dog which is dangerous for tearing runaway negroes; I will chain him here until I capture your boy."

The hunter blew his horn which gathered his dogs, chained the one he spoke of, then he and Mr. Clarkson started on a chase for the runaway slave, who, secreted in the house, had heard every word they had said about him.

After the hunter and Mr. Clarkson had gone, Mrs. Clarkson went to her room (as a general thing the southern mistresses hardly ever knew what went on in their dining rooms and kitchens after meal hours), and Isom, the runaway slave, sat at the same table and ate his breakfast.

After two or three days of vain search in the woods for the runaway slave, Mr. Clarkson asked some of the other negroes on the plantation, if they saw him, to tell him if he came home he would not whip him. Of course, as a general thing, when they stayed in the woods until they were captured, they were whipped but they were not when they came home themselves. One morning after several days of fruitless search in the woods for the runaway slave by the overseer and the hunter, while at breakfast, Isom came up to the door. As soon as Mr. Clarkson learned that the runaway slave was at the door he got up from his breakfast and went out.

"Well, Isom," said Mr. Clarkson. "Well, Massa Thomas," said Isom. "Where have you been?" said Mr. Clarkson. "I been in the woods, sir," answered Isom. Of course it would not have been well for him to tell Mr. Clarkson that he was hidden and fed right in the house, for it would have made it bad for the other negroes who were house servants, among whom he had a brother and sister.

Mr. Clarkson. "Isom, did you get with some other runaways?" "Yes, sir," said Isom. Of course Isom's answer was in keeping with the belief of Mr. Clarkson that he had got in with some experienced runaway in the woods. "How many were with you?" asked Mr. Clarkson. "Two," answered Isom. "What are their names, and to whom do they belong?" asked Mr. Clarkson. "I don't know, sir," said Isom. "Didn't you ask their names?" said Mr. Clarkson. "No, sir," said Isom. "Can you describe them?" asked Mr. Clarkson. "One is big, like you, and the other was little like the man who was hunting me," said Isom. "Where did you see the hunter?" asked Mr. Clarkson. "In the woods, sir," said Isom. "Isom, do you want something to eat?" asked Mr. Clarkson. "Yes, sir," said Isom. He sent him around to the kitchen and told the cook to give him something to eat.

Mrs. Clarkson thought a great deal of Isom, so while he was in the kitchen eating, she went in and had a long talk with him about how he got along since he had been away, as they supposed.

As I have said, in general, when runaway slaves came home themselves, they were not whipped, but were either handcuffed or put in stocks, and locked up for two or three days.

While Isom was eating and talking with Mrs. Clarkson, Mr. Clarkson appeared at the kitchen door with a pistol in one hand and handcuffs in the other. Mrs. Clarkson said, "What are you going to do, Thomas?" "I want Isom as soon as he is through eating," said Mr. Clarkson. "You are not going to lock him up, are you Thomas?" said Mrs. Clarkson. Mrs. Clarkson's name was Henrietta, but her pet name was Henie. Mr. Clarkson said. "Henie, I shan't hurt Isom."

Isom, who had a smooth, black, round face, full eyes, white teeth, was a very beautiful negro. When he saw the pistol and handcuffs in Mr. Clarkson's hands, those large eyes of his were stretched so wide, one could see the white, like great sheets in them.

Mrs. Clarkson said, "Thomas, please don't lock up Isom; he won't run away again. You won't, will you Isom?" "No, mamma massie Henie, I won't," said Isom. "Yes, Henie," said Mr. Clarkson, "he says so, but will he not?" "Thomas," said Mrs. Clarkson, "I will take the responsibility if you do as I ask you to; I will keep Isom around the house and will assure you that he will not run away."

Mr. Clarkson wanted to lock Isom up very much, but he knew what a strong will his wife had, and how hard it would be to get her right when she had got wrong, hence he complied with her request. So Isom worked around the house for a long time. The hunter was to rest a few days, and then resume his work, but Mr. Clarkson wrote to him that his services would be no longer needed, as the runaway slave whom he was employed to hunt had returned himself. I never learned whether the hunter got paid for what he had done.

MR. BLACK, THE SLAVE HUNTER.

There was a white man in Richland County, South Carolina, named Mr. Black, who made his living by hunting runaway slaves. I knew him as well as I did one of my fellow negroes on Col. Singleton's plantation. He was of dark complexion, short stature, spare built, with long, jet black, coarse hair. He bore the description of what some would call a good man, but he was quite the reverse; he was one of the most heartless men I have ever seen.

Mr. Black was a very successful hunter, although sometimes all of his bloodhounds were killed by runaway slaves, and he barely escaped with his life. He used to ride a small bay mare in hunting, which was the only horse he owned. She was a thin, raw-boned creature and looked as though she could hardly walk, but knew the business about as well as her master; and in such troubles as above stated she used to carry him pretty fast out of danger. Mr. Black caught several runaway slaves belonging to Col. Singleton.

I have known him to chase runaway slaves out of the forest right through the colonel's plantation, through a crowd of other negroes, and his dogs would never mistake any among the crowd for the ones they were after. When these hound dogs chased the runaways through farms in that way, many of them were killed and buried in the cotton or corn field by some among the crowd of negroes through which they passed. In general the slaves hated bloodhounds, and would kill them any time they got a chance, but especially on such occasions as above stated, to keep them from capturing runaways.

Once eight slaves ran away from Col. Singleton's plantation, and Mr. Black, with twenty-five hound dogs, was hired to hunt them up. The dogs struck trail of the runaways late one afternoon, and chased them all that night, during which time they got scattered. Next morning three of the runaways were chased through a crowd of their fellow negroes, who were working in the cotton field. While chasing the runaways some among the crowd killed six of the dogs, including the two leading ones, and buried them in the cotton beds or rows, as we used to call them.

Mr. Black, the hunter, though a mile or more off, knew that something had happened from the irregular barking of the other dogs, and also because he did not hear the yelling of the two leading dogs. So he blew his horn, called the rest of his dogs, and gave up the chase until he had replaced his leading dogs by others, which he always had on hand at home.

Slave hunters generally had one or two among the pack of hound dogs, called trailers or leaders, which the others, fifty or more, were trained to follow. So if anything happened to the leaders while on chase, the rest would become confused, and could not follow the runaway. But if the leaders were hurt or killed after the runaways were captured, the rest would surround and guard them until the hunter reached them, as he was always a mile or more behind.

After the leading dogs had been replaced, Mr. Black resumed the chase, and caught some of the runaways, but the rest came home themselves.

The last runaway slave Mr. Black was hired to hunt belonged to Col. M.R. Singleton, and was named Dick, but instead of Dick he caught a slave belonging to a man in Sumterville county, who had been in the woods seven years. This runaway slave had another name at home, but while in the woods had assumed the name of Champion, for his success in keeping slave hunters from capturing him up to that time.

Mr. Black, the hunter, chased Dick and Champion two days and nights; on the morning before the capture of the latter they swam across the Water-ree river. After they got across they were separated; the dogs followed Champion, and ran him down that morning about eleven o'clock. Champion had a gun and pistol; as the first dog ran up and opened his mouth to take hold of him he discharged the contents of the pistol in his mouth and killed him instantly. The rest of the dogs did not take hold of him, but surrounded him and held him at bay until the hunter reached the spot.

When Mr. Black rode up within gunshot, Champion aimed at him with a loaded double barrel gun, but the caps of both barrels snapped from being wet by running through the bushes. Mr. Black had a gun and pistol, too; he attempted to shoot the negro, but William Turner, Col. Singleton's overseer, who hired Mr. Black to hunt Dick, the runaway from the colonel's plantation, would not let him do it. Mr. Black then attempted to strike Champion with the breech of his gun, but Champion kicked him down, and as he drew his knife to stab Mr. Black, Mr. Turner, the overseer, struck him on the back of his head with the butt of a loaded whip. This stunned him for a few moments, and by the time he had regained his senses they had handcuffed him.

After the negro had been handcuffed, Mr. Black wanted to abuse him, because he had killed the dog, and attempted to shoot him, but Mr. Turner, the overseer, would not let him. Champion was taken to Col. Singleton's plantation, locked up in the dungeon under the overseer's house, and his master was notified of his capture; he was a mulatto negro, and his master, who was his father, sent for him at Col. Singleton's plantation; but I never learned whether Mr. Black, the hunter, was ever paid for capturing him. Dick, the runaway negro from Col. Singleton's place, came home himself sometime after Champion, his companion, had been captured.

Mr. Black, the slave hunter, was very poor, and had a large family; he had a wife, with eight or ten helpless children, whom I knew as well as I did my fellow negroes on the colonel's plantation. But as cruel as Mr. Black was to runaway slaves, his family was almost wholly supported by negroes; I have known in some cases that they stole from their masters to help this family. The negroes were so kind to Mr. Black's family that his wife turned against him for his cruelty to runaway slaves.

I have stated that some of the masters and overseers hired the hunters, on condition that they would capture and return the runaway slaves, unbruised and untorn by their dogs; while others, in a mad fit of passion, would say to them, "I want you to bring my runaway nigger home, dead or alive."

All of the slave hunters used to practice cruelty upon the runaway slaves; more especially upon those whose masters would say to hunters "bring them dead or alive." But among all the slave hunters in the part of South Carolina where the author of this work lived, Mr. Black was the most cruel.

It was rumored that many of the runaway slaves that were never heard of afterward, were captured and killed in the woods by Mr. Black, but no special clue to this could be found. Finally Mr. Black was hired to capture a runaway slave in Barnwell County, S.C. This slave was with another, who was thought well of by his master, but hated by the overseer. In the chase, the two runaways separated, and the dogs followed the second instead of the one whom Mr. Black had been hired to hunt. Mr. Black had another hunter with him by the name of Motley. The negro killed several of the dogs, and gave Messrs. Black and Motley a hard fight. After the negro had been captured, they killed him, cut him up and gave his remains to the living dogs.

The companion of the murdered slave was not caught. A few days after the chase, while wandering around in the wood in a somewhat excited state, he came to a spot where the bushes and leaves seemed to have been in a stirred-up condition, as though there had been tussling by two parties. On looking around in this disordered spot, he found pieces of clothing here and there in rags, looking just like the suit worn by his companion, who was then a victim of a most cruel death from the hands of the hunters. On closer examination, he saw spots of blood here and there upon the leaves, which awakened his suspicion; on looking a little way from this spot, he saw some leaves which looked as though they had been moved by hands and put there, and on removing the leaves, he found that the earth had been freshly dug and filled in again. Digging down in the spot, he soon discovered pieces of the person of a dead man, whom he could not identify, but was satisfied that it was the remains of his companion, from whom he had been compelled to separate a few days before. This sight frightened the runaway negro so, that he left the woods, went home to his master and told the story; but as a negro's word was not to be taken against a white man's in the days of slavery, no special notice was taken of what he had said. Still some of the white people were secretly watching Mr. Black, the slave hunter, as he had been before suspected of killing runaway slaves in the woods.

The master of the murdered negro was still ignorant of his death; he was in hopes that his slave would return. But finding that his slave did not return as expected, the master became uneasy, and offered a reward to any one who could give a clue of his negro. In the meantime, he discharged the overseer who had been the cause of his slave running away; and he also kept the overseer's salary of four hundred dollars, which was the annual pay for overseeing his plantation.

Mr. Black's house was in Richland county, and as he was the last who had hunted runaway slaves in Barnwell county before the murder, suspicion rested on him. Still no one said anything to him, but he was very closely watched by men of his own county, whose interest was not in the hatefulness of the crime committed, but rather in the reward offered by the master to any who could give information of his runaway slave.

Sometime after the case had occurred, another white man of Richland county became quite a friend to Mr. Black, the slave hunter; this apparent friendship soon led Mr. Black to tell the secret, which speedily brought him to trial. While he and his pretended friend were on a drinking spree, in the midst of the merriment,--of course the conversation was how to control negroes, as that was the principal topic of the poor white men South, in the days of slavery.

In the conversation, this friend spoke of several plans which he said, if properly carried out, "would keep a nigger in his place." After the friend had said so much to Mr. Black, the slave hunter, the latter felt that he could tell his secret without endangering himself, so he answered: "The way to show a nigger that would resist a white man, his place, is to put him among the missing. Not long since, I went to Barnwell county to hunt a runaway nigger, and my dogs struck trail of another instead of the one I wanted to capture. After quite a long chase my dogs ran him down, and before I reached him he killed several of them, and gave me a hard fight when I got to him. Motley and I were together; I shot him down, and Motley and I cut him up and gave the pieces to the remainder of my dogs; that is the way I put a nigger in his place."

After the secret had been revealed, Mr. Black's friend excused himself, and the former saw him no more until he appeared as a witness against him. The companion of the murdered negro was summoned to carry the investigating party, including the murderer, to the spot where his companion had been buried.

Mr. Black was tried and found to be guilty. After sentence had been passed, he confessed the commission of that crime, and also told that he had killed several runaway negroes previously in his own county. So Mr. Black and Motley, his companion, were both hanged in Barnwell county, S.C. The system of slavery outlived Mr. Black, the slave hunter, just six years.

MANNING BROWN AND AUNT BETTY.

A man by the name of Manning Brown was nursed by an old colored woman he called mamma Betty. She was naturally good natured and a devout Christian, and Mr. Brown gained many of her good qualities when he was under her entire control, at which time he was said to be a boy of very fine sense of feeling and quite promising. But when approaching manhood Mr. Brown fell among a class of other white men who, in the days of slavery, were unbridled in their habits. With this class of men he began to drink, and step by step in this rapid stride he soon became a confirmed drunkard. This habit so over-coated the good influence he had gained from the colored woman, that it rendered him dangerous not only to his enemies, but also to his friends.

Manning Brown was feared by most of the other white men in Richland county, S.C., and, strange to say, although he was dangerous to white men, yet he never lost the respect he had for colored people in his boyhood days. He ate, drank and slept among colored people after he was a grown man, and in many cases when other white men, who were called patrols, caught colored people away from home without tickets, and were about to whip them, Mr. Brown would ride up and say, "The first man who raises a whip at one of those negroes I will blow his brains out." Knowing that he would shoot a man as quick as he would a bird, even if ten patrols were together, when Mr. Brown made such threats, they never would attempt to whip the negroes.

Mr. Brown owned a plantation with forty slaves on it; his good treatment of them enabled him to get more work out of them than most owners got out of their slaves. His slaves thought so much of their "Massa Manning," as they used to call him, that they did everything in their power to please him. But while he was so good to colored people, he was dangerous to many of the white people and feared by them.

A man by the name of Peter Gafney fought a duel with his brother-in-law, whose name was Dr. Kay; the former, who was quite a marksman, was killed by the latter, who was considered a very poor one. This led many who were in favor of Mr. Gafney to feel that there had been foul play by Dr. Ray, the contestant. Mr. Brown, who acted as a second for Mr. Gafney in the fight, felt the loss of his old friend very deeply. A short time after this he sent a challenge to Dr. Ray, stating, "You may either meet me at a certain time, on the spot where you killed P.T. Gafney, for a duel, or I will shoot you on first sight wherever I meet you. Yours, M. Brown."

But Dr. Ray refused in the face of the threat to accept the challenge. Knowing the disposition of Mr. Brown, the people in that county were inflamed with excitement, because the doctor was liable at any moment while riding in the road to be killed. In fear of meeting Mr. Brown, the doctor gave up visiting the most of his sick patients, and almost wholly confined himself to his large plantation. At the same time Mr. Brown was closely watched by his friends to keep him from waylaying the doctor.

A short time after this threat Mr. Brown commenced to drink harder than ever, so that at times he did not know his own family. But the providence of God was slowly leading Mr. Brown through the unknown paths to a sudden change of life, as we shall soon see.

Mr. Brown's family consisted of a wife, one child, and Aunt Betty, the old colored woman who had brought him up. She was the only mother he knew, for his own mother had died when he was an infant, and her dying request had been that mamma Betty, the old woman, should bring up this boy, who was an only child; and when Mr. Brown got married he took Aunt Betty into his family and told her she need not do any work only what she chose to do, and that he would take care of her the balance of her days. And Mrs. Brown regarded Aunt Betty more as a mother-in-law than as a negress servant. Sometimes when Mr. Brown would not listen to his wife, he would to his mamma Betty, when he was sober enough to know her. One afternoon, while Mr. Brown was in one of those drunken fits, he went into his bedroom and lay down across the bed, talking to himself. His wife went in to speak to him, but as she entered he jumped up and got his loaded double barrelled gun and threatened to shoot her. Frightened at this, she ran out of the room and screamed saying, "Oh my God, mamma Betty, please go in and speak to your Massa Manning, for he threatened to shoot me." With that old familiar confidence in one who had often listened to her advice, Aunt Betty went into the house and to the room where she found Mr. Brown lying across the bed, with the gun by his side. On entering the room, as she was advancing toward the bed, she said, "Massa Manning, what is the matter with you? You naughty boy, what is the matter?" On saying these words, before she had reached the bed, Mr. Brown rose, with the gun in hand, and discharged the contents of both barrels at the old woman; she dropped instantly to the floor. Mr. Brown lay across the bed as before, with the gun by his side, talking to himself, and soon dropped to sleep. Mrs. Brown fainted away several times under the excitement.

Aunt Betty lived about an hour. Soon after she had been shot she wanted to see Mr. Brown, but when told that she could not, she said, "O, my Lord, I wanted to see my child before I die, and I know that he would want to see his mamma Betty, too, before she leaves him." During the time she lived she prayed for Mr. Brown, and requested that he would change his course of life, become a Christian, and meet her in heaven. After singing one of her familiar hymns, Aunt Betty said to some one who stood by her bedside, "I want you to tell Massa Manning that he must not feel bad for what he did to me, because I know that if he was in his right mind he would not hurt me any more than he would himself. Tell him that I have prayed to the Lord for him that he may be a good boy, and I want him to promise that he will be a Christian and meet me in heaven." With these words Aunt Betty became speechless, dying a few moments afterwards. The doctor was sent for, but had to come from such a distance that she died before he reached there.

When Mr. Brown awoke from his drunken state in the night, and learned the sad news of Aunt Betty's death, of which he had been the cause, he clasped his hands and cried out, "What! is it possible that my mamma Betty, the only mother I ever knew, was killed by my hands?" He ran into the room where the corpse was and clasped the remains of the old negress in his arms and cried, "Mamma Betty, mamma Betty, please speak to me as you used to." But that voice was hushed in death.

The doctor, overseer and others tried to quiet him, but they could not. That night Mr. Brown took the train to Columbia, the capital of South Carolina, and gave himself up to the law next day. He was told that it was all right; that the old negress was his slave. But Mr. Brown was dissatisfied; he came back home and invited all the white neighbors and slaves to Aunt Betty's funeral, in which he and his family took part. After the excitement was over the message of Aunt Betty was delivered to Mr. Brown; he was told that her last request had been that he would meet her in heaven. He answered, "I will." Mr. Brown then and there took an oath that he would drink no more strong drinks. He then disposed of his slaves, but how I did not learn. Soon after this he was converted and became one of the ablest preachers in Richland county, S.C. Mr. Brown's conversion freed Dr. Ray from his threat. The doctor was so glad of this that he paid quite a large sum towards Mr. Brown's salary for preaching.

CHAPTER III

CHAPTER III.--MY EXPERIENCE IN THE CIVIL WAR.

My knowledge of the Civil War, extends from the time when the first gun was fired on Fort Sumter in April, 1861, to the close of the War.

While the slaves were not pressed into the Confederate service as soldiers, yet they were used in all the slave-holding states at war points, not only to build fortifications, but also to work on vessels used in the war.

The slaves were gathered in each state, anywhere from 6000 to 8000 or more, from different plantations, carried to some centre and sent to various war points in the state.

It would be impossible to describe the intense excitement which prevailed among the Confederates in their united efforts to raise troops to meet the Union forces. They were loud in their expressions of the certainty of victory.

Many of the poor white men were encouraged by the promise of from three to five negroes to each man who would serve in the Confederate service, when the Confederate government should have gained the victory.

On the other hand, the negroes were threatened with an increase of the galling yoke of slavery. These threats were made with significant expressions, and the strongest assumption that the negro was the direct cause of the war.

HOW SLAVES WERE GATHERED AND CARRIED TO WAR POINTS.

No sooner had the war commenced in the spring of 1861, than the slaves were gathered from the various plantations, and shipped by freight cars, or boats, to some centre, and apportioned out and sent to work at different war points. I do not know just how many slaves the Confederate Government required each master to furnish for its service, but I know that 15 of the 465 slaves on my master's, Col. M.E. Singleton's, plantation, were sent to work on fortifications each year during the war.

The war had been going on two years before my turn came. In the summer of 1863 with thousands of other negroes, gathered from the various parts of the state, I was freighted to the city of Charleston, South Carolina, and the group in which my lot fell was sent to Sullivan's Island. We were taken on a boat from the city of Charleston, and landed in a little village, situated nearly opposite Fort Sumter, on this island. Leaving behind us Fort Moultrie, Fort Beauregard, and several small batteries, we marched down the white sandy beach of the island, below Fort Marshall, to the very extreme point, where a little inlet of water divides Sullivan's from Long Island, and here we were quartered under Capt. Charles Haskell.

From this point on the island, turning our faces northward, with Morris Island northwest of us, and looking directly north out into the channel, we saw a number of Union gun boats, like a flock of black sheep feeding on a plain of grass; while the men pacing their decks looked like faithful shepherds watching the flock. While we negroes remained upon Sullivan's Island, we watched every movement of the Union fleet, with hearts of joy to think that they were a part of the means by which the liberty of four and one-half millions of slaves was to be effected in accordance with the emancipation proclamation made the January preceding. We kept such close watch upon them that some one among us, whether it was night or day, would be sure to see the discharge of a shot from the gun boat before the sound of the report was heard. During that summer there was no engagement between the Union fleet and the Confederates at that point in South Carolina. The Union gun boats, however, fired occasional shots over us, six miles, into the city of Charleston. They also fired a few shells into a marsh between Sullivan's Island and Mount Pleasant, but with no damage to us.

WHAT WORK THE NEGROES DID ON THE ISLAND.

After we had reached the island, our company was divided. One part was quartered at one end of the Island, around Fort Moultrie, and we were quartered at the other end, at Fort Marshall. Our work was to repair forts, build batteries, mount guns, and arrange them. While the men were engaged at such work, the boys of my age, namely, thirteen, and some older, waited on officers and carried water for the men at work, and in general acted as messengers between different points on the island.

ENGAGEMENT ON LONG ISLAND.

Though there was no fighting on Sullivan's Island during my stay there, Confederate soldiers at times crossed the inlet from Sullivan's to Long Island, in the night and engaged in skirmishes with Union soldiers, who had entered the upper end of that island and camped there. Whether these Confederate scouts were ever successful in routing the Union forces on the island or not I have never learned, but I know that they were several times repulsed with considerable loss.

NEGROES ESCAPE.

The way the Confederates came to the knowledge that Union soldiers were on Long Island was that the group of negroes who preceded us on Sullivan's Island had found out that Union soldiers were camping on the upper end of Long Island. So one night quite a number of them escaped by swimming across the inlet that divides Sullivan's Island and Long Island, and succeeded in reaching the Union line.

The next day it was discovered that they had swam across the inlet, and the following night they were pursued by a number of Confederate scouts who crossed in a flat boat. Instead of the capture of the negroes, who would have been victims of the most cruel death, the Confederate scouts were met by soldiers from the Union line, and after a hot engagement they were repulsed, as they usually were.

BUILDING A BATTERY ON LONG ISLAND.

Finally the Confederates took a large number of the group of which I was a member from Sullivan's to the south shore of Long Island and there built a battery, and mounted several small field guns upon it. As they were afraid of being discovered in the daytime we were obliged to work on the battery nights and were taken back to Sullivan's in the morning, until the work was completed.

We were guarded by Confederate soldiers while building the battery, as, without a guard it would have been easy for any of us to have reached the Union line on the north end of Long Island. Sullivan's Island was about five miles long.

A NEGRO SERVANT MURDERED.

One of the most heartless deeds committed while I was on Sullivan's Island, was that of the murder of a negro boy by his master, a Confederate officer to whom the boy had been a body servant. What the rank of this officer was I am not sure, but I think he was a Major, and that he was from the state of Georgia. It was a common thing for southern men to carry dirks, especially during the war. This officer had one, and for something the boy displeased him in, he drew the knife and made a fatal stab between the boy's collar bone and left shoulder. As the victim fell at the brutal master's feet, we negroes who had witnessed the fiendish and cowardly act upon a helpless member of our race, expected an immediate interference from the hand of justice in some form or other. But we looked and waited in vain, for the horrible deed did not seem to have changed the manner of those in authority in the least, but they rather treated it as coolly as though nothing had happened. Finding that the Confederates failed to lay the hand of justice upon the officer, we, with our vague ideas of moral justice, and with our extreme confidence that God would somehow do more for the oppressed negroes than he would ordinarily for any other people, anxiously waited a short time for some token of Divine vengeance, but as we found that no such token as we desired, in the heat of our passion, came, we finally concluded to wait God's way and time, as to how, and when this, as every other wrong act, should be visited with his unfailing justice.

But aside from this case we fared better on these fortifications than we had at home on the plantations. This was the case at least with those of us who were on Sullivan's Island. Our work in general on the fortifications was not hard, we had a great deal of spare time, and although we knew that our work in the Confederate service was against our liberty, yet we were delighted to be in military service.

We felt an exalted pride that, having spent a little time at these war points, we had gained some knowledge which would put us beyond our fellow negroes at home on the plantations, while they would increase our pride by crediting us with far more knowledge than it was possible for us to have gained.

Our daily rations from the Commissary was a quart of rice or hard-tack, and a half pound of salt pork or corn-beef.

The change from the cabins and from the labor on the old plantations so filled our cup of joy that we were sorry when the two months of our stay on the island was ended.

At the end of about two months, I, with the rest of my fellow negroes of that group, was sent back to the plantation again, while others took our places.

MY EXPERIENCE IN FORT SUMTER.

In the summer of 1864, when I was in my fourteenth year, another call was made for negro laborers for the Confederate government, and fifteen from our plantation, including myself, with thousands from other plantations, were sent down to Charleston again.

There the negroes were apportioned in groups to be sent to the different fortifications. My lot fell among the group of three hundred and sixty, who were assigned to Fort Sumter. I shall never forget with what care they had to move in carrying us in a steamer from the government wharf in Charleston to John's island wharf, on account of the network of torpedo mines in Charleston Harbor.

From John's island wharf they carried us in rowboats to Fort Sumter, and, as those boats could not carry many, it took all night to convey us with other freightage to Fort Sumter.

The steamer which carried us from Charleston to John's island wharf had to run at night. Indeed every move the Confederates made about there near the close of the war had to be made at night because the Yankees on gunboats outside the channel and those on Morris island kept so close a watch it was very dangerous to convey us from John's island wharf to Fort Sumter because the oars dipping into the salt water at night made sparks like fire, and thus the Yankees on Morris island were able to see us. Indeed their shots oftentimes took effect.

Many of the negroes were killed. Of the fifteen from our plantation, one boy of about my age was struck by a parrot shell while climbing from the boat into the fort. We were told of the perils we were to meet, both before and after we reached our destination. For one of the most disheartening things was the sad report of the survivors of those whose places we were to fill. As the rowboats left them on John's island wharf and as we were about to embark they told us of the great danger to which we would be exposed,--of the liability of some of us being killed before we reached the fort, which proved true, and of how fast their comrades were killed in Fort Sumter. A number, it was said, died from fright before reaching Sumter.

THE OFFICERS AND QUARTERS.

The officers who were then in command of the fort were Capt. J.C. Mitchell and Major John Johnson. The name of the overseer in charge of the negroes in the fort was Deburgh,--whether that was his right name I can not say.

Deburgh was a foreigner by birth. He was one of the most cruel men I ever knew. As he and his atrocious deeds will come up later in this history, I will say no more of him here.

CONDITION OF THE FORT.

Fort Sumter, which previous to this, had not only been silenced by the Union forces, but also partly demolished, had but one gun mounted on it, on the west side. That cannon we used to call the "Sundown Gun," because it was fired every evening as the sun went down,--as well as at sunrise. On this west side the Confederate officers and soldiers were sheltered in the bomb-proof safe during bombardment. On the east side of the fort, facing Morris island, opposite Fort Wagner, there was another apartment called the "Rat-hole" in which we negroes were quartered.

WHAT THE NEGROES DID IN FORT SUMTER.

Fort Sumter had been so badly damaged by the Union forces in 1863, that unless something had been done upon the top, the continued bombardment which it suffered up to the close of the war, would have rendered it uninhabitable.

The fort was being fired upon every five minutes with mortar and parrot shells by the Yankees from Morris Island.

The principal work of the negroes was to secure the top and other parts against the damage from the Union guns.

Large timbers were put on the rampart of the fort, and boards laid on them, then baskets, without bottoms, about two feet wide, and four feet high, were put close together on the rampart, and filled with sand by the negroes.

The work could only be done at night, because, besides the bombardment from Fort Wagner which was about a mile or little less from us, there were also sharp-shooters there who picked men off whenever they showed their heads on the rampart.

The mortar and parrot shells rained alternately upon Fort Sumter every five minutes, day and night, but the sharp-shooters could only fire by day-light.

The negroes were principally exposed to the bombardment. The only time the few Confederate soldiers were exposed to danger was while they were putting the Chevaldefrise on the parapet at night.

The "Chevaldefrise" is a piece of timber with wooden spikes pointed with iron, and used for defence on fortifications.

In the late war between the Spaniards and the Americans, the former used barbed wire for the same purpose.

If my readers could have been in Fort Sumter in the summer of 1864 they would have heard the sentinel cry, every five minutes, "Look out! Mortar!" Then they would have seen the negroes running about in the fort yard in a confused state, seeking places of safety from the missile sure to bring death to one or more of them. Another five minutes, and again the cry of the sentinel, "Look out," means a parrot shell, which is far more deadly than is the mortar because it comes so quickly that one has no chance to seek a place of safety.

The next moment the survivors of us, expecting that it would be our turn next, would be picking up, here and there, parts of the severed bodies of our fellow negroes; many of those bodies so mutilated as not to be recognizable.

DEBURGH, THE OVERSEER.

Deburgh, the overseer, of whom I have spoken, was a small man, of light complexion, and very light hair.

If my readers could have been in Fort Sumter in July, 1864, they would have seen Deburgh with a small bar of iron or a piece of shell in his hand, forcing the surviving portion of the negroes back into line and adding to these, other negroes kept in the Rat-hole as reserves to fill the places of those who were killed and wounded.

They would also have heard him swearing at the top of his voice, while forcing the negroes to rearrange themselves in line from the base of the fort to the top.

This arrangement of the negroes, enabled them to sling to each other the bags of sand which was put in the baskets on the top of the fort. My readers ask, what was the sand put on the fort for? It was to smother the fuses of such shells as reached the ramparts before bursting.

After the bombardment of Port Sumter in 1863, by the Union forces, its top of fourteen or sixteen feet in thickness, built of New Hampshire granite, was left bare. From that time all through 1864, the shells were so aimed as to burst right over the fort; and it was pieces of these shells which flew in every direction that were so destructive.

The fuses of many of these shells fired on Port Sumter did not burn in time to cause the shells to burst before falling. Now as the shells fell on the rampart of the fort instead of falling and bursting on the stone, they buried themselves harmlessly in the sand, which put out the fuse and also kept them from bursting.

But while the destruction of life was lessened by the sand, it was fully made up by the hand of that brute, the overseer. God only knows how many negroes he killed in Port Sumter under the shadow of night. Every one he reached, while forcing the slaves back into working position after they had been scattered by the shells, he would strike on the head with the piece of iron he carried in his hand, and, as his victim fell, would cry out to some other negro, "Put that fellow in his box," meaning his coffin.

Whether the superior officers in Fort Sumter knew that Deburgh was killing the negroes off almost as fast as the shells from Fort Wagner, or whether they did not know, and did not care, I never have learned. But I have every reason to believe that one of them at least, namely, Major John Johnson, would not have allowed such a wholesale slaughter, had he known. On the other hand I believe that Capt. J.C. Mitchell was not only mean enough to have allowed it, but that he was fully as heartless himself.

Whatever became of Deburgh, whether he was killed in Fort Sumter or not, I never knew.

OUR SUPERIOR OFFICERS.

The two officers in command of Fort Sumter in July of 1864 were Capt. J.C. Mitchell, and Major John Johnson.

Major Johnson was as kind, gentle, and humane to the negroes as could have been expected.

On the other hand, the actions of Capt. Mitchell were harsh and very cruel. He had a bitter hatred toward the Yankees, and during the rain of shells on Fort Sumter, he sought every opportunity to expose the negroes to as much danger as he dared.

I remember that one night Capt. Mitchell ordered us outside of Fort Sumter to a projection of the stone-bed upon which the Fort was built, right in front of Fort Wagner. At that place we were in far greater danger from the deadly missiles of the Union forces than we were exposed to on the inside of Sumter, and I could see no other reasons for his ordering us outside of the fort that night than that we might be killed off faster.

It seems that during the incessant firing on Fort Sumter the officers held a consultation as to whether it was not best to evacuate the fort.

It was at this time that it was rumored,--a rumor that we had every reason to believe,--that Capt. Mitchell plotted to lock us negroes up in our quarters in Sumter, known as the Rat-hole; and put powder to it and arrange it so that both the negroes and the Yankees should be blown up, when the latter should have taken possession after the evacuation of the fort by the Confederates.

But we learned that Major John Johnson, who has since become an Episcopal minister, in Charleston, S.C., wholly refused to agree with Capt. Mitchell in such a barbarous and cowardly act, and, as though Providence were watching over the innocent and oppressed negroes, and over the Yankees as well, because they were fighting in a righteous cause, Capt. Mitchell's career and further chances of carrying out his cruel intentions were cut short. He was mortally wounded by the sharp-shooters of Fort Wagner, on the 14th of July, 1864, and died four hours afterwards.

OUR RATIONS IN SUMTER.

The working forces of negroes in Sumter with the exception of the boys who carried messages to the different parts of the fort day and night, were locked up days, and turned out nights, to work. We drew our rations of hard-tack and salt pork twice a day; mornings when we ceased work and turned in for the day, and again, between three and four o'clock in the afternoon, so as to have supper eaten in time to go to work at dark.

We often ate our salt pork raw with the hard-tack, as there were no special means of cooking in the negroes' apartment. We were not only in danger, while at work, from the continued rain of shells, but oftentimes when we were put in line to draw our rations some of us were killed or wounded.

I cannot say how they got fresh water in Fort Sumter, as I do not remember seeing any brought there in boats, neither did I notice any conveniences there for the catching of rain water.

The water we negroes used was kept in large hogsheads with coal tar in them; I do not know what the tar was put in the water for unless it was for our health. The "rat-hole" into which we were locked, was like a sweat box; it was so hot and close, that, although we were exposed to death by shells when we were turned out to work, we were glad to get into the fresh air.

We had little cups in which they used to give us whiskey mornings when we went in, and again when we were going out to work at night.

I don't know how many of the forty survivors of the three hundred and sixty of us who were carried into the Fort in the summer of 1864 besides myself are still alive. But if there are any with the keen tenderness of a negro, they cannot help joining me in an undying sense of gratitude to Major John Johnson, not only for his kind and gentle dealings with us which meant so much to a negro in the days of slavery, but also for his humane protection, which saved us from some of the danger from shells to which we were exposed in Sumter.

A short time after Capt. J.C. Mitchell had been killed, Major Johnson was dangerously wounded in the head by a piece of shell.

MY LAST NIGHT IN FORT SUMTER AND THE GLORIOUS END OF THE WAR.

During the time we spent in Fort Sumter we had not seen a clear day or night. In harmony with the continual danger by which we were surrounded, the very atmosphere wore the pall of death; for it was always rainy and cloudy. The mutilated bodies of the negroes, mingled with the black mud and water in the fort yard, added to the awfulness of the scene. Pieces of bombshells and other pieces of iron, and also large southern pine timbers were scattered all over the yard of the fort. There was also a little lime house in the middle of the yard, into which we were warned not to go when seeking places of safety from the deadly missiles at the cry of the sentinel.

The orders were that we should get as near the centre of the fort yard as possible and lie down. The reason for this was that the shells which were fired upon Sumter were so measured that they would burst in the air, and the pieces would generally fly toward the sides of the fort. But the orders were not strictly carried out, because, at the warning cries of the sentinel, we became confused. That night, at the cry of the sentinel, I ran and lay down on one of the large southern pine timbers, and several of my fellow negroes followed and piled in upon me. Their weight was so heavy that I cried out as for life. The sense of that crush I feel at certain times even now.

At the next report of a shell I ran toward the lime house, but some one tripped me up, and, by the time I had got to my feet again, twelve or thirteen others were crowded into it. Another negro and I reached the doorway, but we were not more than there before a mortar shell came crushing down upon the little lime house, and all within were so mangled that their bodies were not recognizable.

Only we two were saved. My companion had one of his legs broken, and a piece of shell had wounded me over my right eye and cut open my under lip. At the moment I was wounded I was not unconscious, but I did not know what had hurt me. I became almost blind from the effect of my wounds, but not directly after I was wounded, and I felt no pain for a day or so. With other wounded I was taken to the bombproof in the fort. I shall never forget this first and last visit to the hospital department. To witness the rough handling of the wounded patients, to see them thrown on a table as one would a piece of beef, and to see the doctor use his knife and saw, cutting off a leg, or arm, and sometimes both, with as much indifference as if he were simply cutting up beef, and to hear the doctor say, of almost every other one of these victims, after a leg or an arm was amputated, "Put that fellow in his box," meaning his coffin, was an awful experience. After the surgeon had asked to whom I belonged, he dressed my wounds.

My readers will remember that I stated that no big boat could run to Fort Sumter at that time, on account of the bombardment. We had to be conveyed back to John's Island wharf in rowboats, which was the nearest distance a steamer could go to Fort Sumter.

As one of those rowboats was pushed out to take the dead and wounded from the fort, and as the for men were put into the boat, which was generally done before they put in the latter, fortunately, just before the wounded were put in, a Parrott shell was fired into it from Fort Wagner by the Union forces, which sunk both the boat and the coffins, with their remains.

My readers would ask how the Confederates disposed of the negroes who were killed in Fort Sumter. Those who were not too badly mutilated were sent over to the city of Charleston and were buried in a place which was set apart to bury the negroes. But others, who were so badly cut up by shells, were put into boxes, with pieces of iron in them, and carried out a little away from Sumter and thrown overboard.

I was then taken to John's Island wharf, and from there to the city of Charleston in a steamer, and carried to Doctor Rag's hospital, where I stopped until September. Then I was sent back home to my master's plantation. Quoting the exact words of Major John Johnson, a Confederate officer under whom I was a part of the time at the above-named place, I would say: "July 7th, Fort Sumter's third great bombardment, lasting sixty days and nights, with a total of 14,666 rounds fired at the fort, with eighty-one casualties."

WHAT TOOK PLACE AFTER.

I said that after I got well enough to travel I was sent back home to my master's plantation, about a hundred miles from the city of Charleston, in central South Carolina. This was in September of 1864, and I, with the rest of my fellow-negroes on this extensive plantation, and with other slaves all over the South, were held in suspense waiting the final outcome of the emancipation proclamation, issued January, 1863, but as the war continued, it had not taken effect until the spring of 1865.

Here I had less work than before the war, for the nearer the war approached its close the less the slaves had to do, as the masters were at the end of their wits what to do. In the latter part of 1864 Gen. Sherman, with his army of a hundred thousand men and almost as many stragglers, covered the space of about sixty miles in width while marching from Georgia through South Carolina. The army camped around Columbia, the capital of South Carolina, for a short time. Early in the spring of 1865 the commissary building first took fire, which soon spread to such extent that the whole city of Columbia was consumed; just a few houses on the suburbs were left.

The commissary building was set on fire by one of the two parties, but it was never fully settled whether it was done by Gen. Sherman's men or by the Confederates, who might have, as surmised by some, as they had to evacuate the city, set it on fire to keep Gen. Sherman's men from getting the food. After this Columbia was occupied by a portion of Sherman's men, while the others marched on toward North Carolina.

THE GLORIOUS END.

In closing this brief sketch of my experiences in the war, I would ask my readers to go back of the war a little with me. I want to show them a few of the dark pictures of the slave system. Hark! I hear the clanking of the ploughman's chains in the fields; I hear the tramping of the feet of the hoe-hands. I hear the coarse and harsh voice of the negro driver and the shrill voice of the white overseer swearing at the slaves. I hear the swash of the lash upon the backs of the unfortunates; I hear them crying for mercy from the merciless. Amidst these cruelties I hear the fathers and mothers pour out their souls in prayer,--"O, Lord, how long!" and their cries not only awaken the sympathy of their white brothers and sisters of the North, but also mightily trouble the slave masters of the South.

The firing on Fort Sumter, in April of 1861, brought hope to the slaves that the long looked for year of jubilee was near at hand. And though the South won victory after victory, and the Union reeled to and fro like a drunken man, the negroes never lost hope, but faithfully supported the Union cause with their prayers.

Thank God, where Christianity exists slavery cannot exist.

At last came freedom. And what joy it brought! I am now standing, in imagination, on a high place just outside the city of Columbia, in the spring of 1865. The stars and stripes float in the air. The sun is just making its appearance from behind the hills, and throwing its beautiful light upon green bush and tree. The mocking birds and jay birds sing this morning more sweetly than ever before. Beneath the flag of liberty there is congregated a perfect network of the emancipated slaves from the different plantations, their swarthy faces, from a distance, looking like the smooth water of a black sea. Their voices, like distant thunder, rend the air,--

> "Old master gone away, and the darkies all at home,
> There must be now the kingdom come and the year of jubilee."

The old men and women, bent over by reason of age and servitude, bound from their staves, praising God for deliverance.

Other American Indian titles offered by *Digital Scanning, Inc.*

The North American Indians
(2 Volume Set)
As Published in 1903.

Volume 1:
TP: 1582182124 ($27.95)
HC: 1582182736 ($39.95)

Volume 2:
TP: 1582182132 ($27.95)
HC: 1582182744 ($39.95)

The Adventures of the Ojibbeway and Ioway Indians
(2 Volume Set)
As Published in 1852.

Volume 1:
TP: 1582184941 ($17.95)
HC: 158218495X ($29.95)

Volume 2:
TP: 1582184984 ($17.95)
HC: 1582184992 ($29.95)

Indian Boyhood
by Charles A. Eastman
As Published in 1902.

TP: 1582186863 ($14.95)
HC: 1582186871 ($28.95)

Massasoit of the Wampanoags
by Alvin G. Weeks
As Published in 1920.

TP: 1582185921 ($14.95)
HC: 158218593X ($27.95)

AB-SA-RA-KA
The Land of Massacre
by Margaret Carrington
As Published in 1879.

TP: 1582183821 ($19.95)
HC: 158218383X ($34.95)

Boots and Saddles
by Elizabeth Custer
As Published in 1885.

TP: 1582181268 ($15.95)
HC: 1582181411 ($25.95)

To order any of the above titles or the titles listed on the back of this page:

- **Contact your local bookstore and order through *Ingram Books*.**
- **Contact the publisher directly (for general information or special event purchases):**

Digital Scanning, Inc.
344 Gannett Rd., Scituate, MA 02066
Phone: (781) 545-2100 Fax: (781) 545-4908 Toll Free in the U.S.: 888-349-4443
email: books@digitalscanning.com
www.digitalscanning.com

Other American Indian titles offered by Digital Scanning, Inc. (cont.):

The Story of the Indian,
by George Bird Grinnell
As Published in 1902.
TP: 1582182450 ($15.95)
HC: 1582182469 ($29.95)

Blackfoot Lodge Tales,
by George Bird Grinnell
As Published in 1892.
TP: 1582185069 ($17.95)
HC: 1582185077 ($30.95)

The Fighting Cheyennes,
by George Bird Grinnell
As Published in 1915.
TP: 1582183902 ($19.95)
HC: 1582183910 ($34.95)

The Soul of the Indian,
by Charles A. Eastman
As Published in 1911.
TP: 1582186405 ($11.95)
HC: 1582186413 ($22.95)

From Deep Woods to Civilization,
by Charles A. Eastman
As Published in 1916.
TP: 1582186162 ($11.95)
HC: 1582186170 ($25.95)

Wigwam Evenings,
by Charles A. Eastman & Elaine Goodale Eastman
As Published in 1909.
TP: 1582186081 ($13.95)
HC: 158218609X ($26.95)

Indian Heroes and Great Chieftains,
by Charles A. Eastman
As Published in 1918.
TP: 1582186006 ($13.95)
HC: 1582186014 ($26.95)

Tenting on the Plains,
by Elizabeth Custer
As Published in 1887.
TP: 1582180504 ($29.95)
HC: 1582180512 ($39.95)

Following the Guidon,
by Elizabeth Custer
As Published in 1890.
TP: 1582181160 ($19.95)
HC: 1582181195 ($29.95)

The Young Reader's Catlin-My Life Among the Indians,
by George Catlin
As Published in 1909.
TP: 158218478X ($19.95)
HC: 1582184798 ($31.95)

The Last of the Great Scouts-The Life of Col. W. F. Cody (Buffalo Bill),
by Helen Cody Wetmore
As Published in 1899.
TP: 1582182019 ($19.95)
HC: 1582182000 ($27.95)

The Old Indian Chronicle,
by Samuel A. Drake
As Published in 1867.
TP: 1582185026 ($17.95)
HC: 1582185034 ($29.95)

The Life of Mary Jemison-The White Woman of the Genesee,
by James E. Seaver
As Published in 1880.
TP: 1582182337 ($15.95)
HC: 1582182345 ($29.95)

Indian Massacre in Minnesota: A History of the Great Massacre by the Sioux,
by Charles S. Bryant & Abel Murch
As Published in 1864.
TP: 1582184100 ($24.95)
HC: 1582184119 ($39.95)

Sheridan's Troopers on the Border,
by De B. Randolph Keim
As Published in 1885.
TP: 1582180601 ($17.95)
HC: 158218061X ($29.95)

A Century of Dishonor,
by Helen Hunt Jackson
As Published in 1889.
TP: 1582182884 ($24.95)
HC: 1582182892 ($39.95)

The Book of the Indians of North America,
by Samuel G. Drake
As Published in 1833.
TP: 1582180946 ($21.95)
HC: 1582181322 ($34.95)

Life Among the Apaches,
by John C. Cremony
As Published in 1868.
TP: 1582183864 ($15.95)
HC: 1582183872 ($29.95)

My Life and Experiences Among Our Hostile Indians,
by Major General O. O. Howard
As Published in 1907.
TP: 1582182604 ($27.95)
HC: 1582182612 ($39.95)

Recent Indian Wars Under the Lead of Sitting Bull,
by James P. Boyd
As Published in 1891.
TP: 1582182183 ($19.95)
HC: 1582182191 ($29.95)

Life of Sitting Bull and History of the Indian War,
by W. Fletcher Johnson
As Published in 1891.
TP: 1582181985 ($27.95)
HC: 1582181977 ($39.95)

Campaigning With Crook,
by Capt. King
As Published in 1899.
TP: 1582183627 ($15.95)
HC: 1582183635 ($29.95)

The History of Philip's War,
by Thomas Church, Esq.
As Published in 1827.
TP: 158218089X ($19.95)
HC: 1582181306 ($29.95)

History of King Philip,
by John Abbott
As Published in 1857.
TP: 1582183147 ($19.95)
HC: 1582183155 ($34.95)

Massacres of the Mountains *(2 Volume Set)*,
by J.P. Dunn, Jr.
As Published in 1886.
Volume 1:
TP: 1582182035 ($19.95)
HC: 1582182752 ($34.95)
Volume 2:
TP: 1582182043 ($19.95)
HC: 1582182760 ($34.95)

The Man Who Married the Moon and Other Pueblo Indian Folk Stories,
by Charles F. Lummis
As Published in 1894.
TP: 1582182698 ($14.95)
HC: 1582182701 ($27.95)

Warpath & Bivouac or Conquest of the Sioux,
by John F. Finnerty
As Published in 1890.
TP: 1582181950 ($24.95)
HC: 1582181942 ($34.95)

CPSIA information can be obtained
at www.ICGtesting.com
Printed in the USA
FFHW021535110419
51647059-57093FF